The Cosmic Purr

Inspiration for Animal Lovers

Karen Craft

Contributing Author

Connery Craft, a cat

This book is dedicated to my husband, David, with gratitude for his patience and support, and to the animal companions—past, present, and future— who grace our lives.

The Cosmic Purr

Inspiration for Animal Lovers

Written and Illustrated by Karen Craft

Contributing Author, Connery Craft, a cat

Interior Layout by Stacey Willey

Edited by David Everett Craft

Copyright 2009 Karen Craft

Published by Animal Shaman Arts

P.O. Box 1998, Ames, IA 50010

Publishing Coordination by
Globe Printing, Inc. Ishpeming, MI
www.globeprinting.net

ISBN 978-0-615-25310-7

First Printing May 2009

With gratitude to....

My editorial board: Roberta Morgan, Valerie Stallbaumer, Kathy Paxson, Leanne Alexander, and especially, Sondy Kaska and Julie Minot (with input from Moonshine).

My booster club: All of the above plus Elaine Robinson, Diana Schmidt, Trish Sheil, Lenore Hamill, Holly Bender, Diana Young, Sharon Schnotala, and the spirit of Steve Irwin.

My parents, Frederick and Margaret Schwartz, and my sister, Mary Lemley, for their financial and emotional support.

My sister, Margaret Candler, and my friend, Jo Myers-Walker, for encouraging my artistic efforts.

Eunice and Everett Craft – Mom and Dad – for cheering me on.

Stacey Willey, for making this project a reality.

Suzette Schmidt, for her invaluable intuitive guidance.

Susan Marie Guenther for starting me on my spiritual path.

My shamanic and healing instructors, Elariel, Phoenix Rising Star, and Jerry Standing Bear White.

My friends/teachers/co-journeyers at Venus Rising:

Linda Star Wolf, Brad Collins, Ruby Falconer, Nita Gage, Windraven, Sundance, Sarah Jane Fridy, Judy Red Hawk, and (of course) Vision-Wolf.

Malabika Shaw for her boundless enthusiasm and for teaching me to use EFT.

My animal communication teachers and mentors:

Susan Marino, Dawn Hayman, Sharon Callahan, and Penelope Smith.

All my beloved animal friends and teachers, including…

The "Dalai Llamas," Corrie and Raindance;

Horses: Deeteza, Gnu, TLC, Jericho, Salute, and Tusk;

Dogs: my own precious pups: Elke, Keeva, Angel, Katie, Tundra, Sky, Natasha and Aspen; and my dogsledding buddy, Burdock;

Cats: my personal companions: Norton, Sunny, Lotus, Misha, and Connery; and my Master Teachers in feline form: Sonya Pia, Lily, and Sherman.

Table of Contents

Heart Talk

"Tigers are not cuddly furred—their coats are stiff and prickly. Better to be like me—the tiger-hearted house cat you can stroke and snuggle up to."

~ Connery, Karen's cat companion

Introducing Connery and Karen

🐾 Connery:

Allow me to introduce myself. In this lifetime, I'm known as Connery (or Mr. C for short), named for a famous actor who, Karen (my co-author and human Mom) assures me, is "suave, but with a twinkle." An entirely appropriate namesake, then.

I arrived on this playing field in the form of a green-eyed, gray-striped cat, born in the shadow of the tiger. Literally. To be certain Karen would sit up and pay attention, I selected a cat mother who lived with a family circus; a real, performing circus, not the newspaper comic strip kind, Karen points out. When Karen first laid eyes on me, my brothers and sister, we were newborn kittens, dreaming in a heap inside a wire crate next to the cage of the tiger who assisted in the magic act. That made an impression on her! (I've found that half the battle with humans is getting them to pay attention.) I promise to fill you in on the details of our meeting in the next chapter.

I came into Karen's life just as she was discovering her talents as an animal communicator—a person who connects telepathically with animals and translates their thoughts and emotions into human words. I'm proud to say I was the very first animal she consciously heard. She received my message so loud and clear that she actually saw it spelled out in front of her eyes in neon-blue capital letters as well as hearing it in her mind. The message was: "TRUST ME."

Karen has known for quite some time that I've wanted to collaborate with her on a book project to share my experiences and offer some friendly advice. As this book unfolds, you may wonder how an illiterate cat can reference literary works and popular media. The explanation is simply that I have access to whatever my human partner has in her awareness. I've been known to watch a little television for myself, as well, at least when I was younger. My consciousness travels with Karen when she attends holistic and spiritual retreats; then I link up with whole communities of humans and animals outside my usual range. All this without leaving the comforts of home. While I can easily perform astral projection, as can any cat worth its salt, it's so much more rewarding to do so in the context of sharing Karen's experiences and plugging into her network of friends and teachers. All part of my curiosity about the discovery and development of spirituality; I learn along with Karen. Likewise, my cat brother, Misha, and I often travel with her on her shamanic journeys into altered states of consciousness.

Now I anticipate your question: "Why would a cat want to write a book to inspire humans?" While there are some cats who don't love anyone, not even themselves (just as there are some people in the same condition, even more people than cats I would venture), most of us house cats love our human companions. You continually amuse, entertain and surprise us. Helping Karen work through her resistance to co-authoring a book with me has been quite an adventure. I once told her, "I can wait for you as patiently as I wait for a mouse," but it has proven to be a challenge. Yet the process has given me far greater insight into the obstacles people create for themselves. Your animal companions would like to help put these obstacles in perspective so you can be happy. When you're happy, we're happy, and it's just that simple.

Part of Karen's resistance to working on this book has been her concern that there are so many self-help/motivational/spiritual advice books already in print, how can we present anything new? From lifetimes of observing human behavior from the cat's eye view, my perception is you people don't always "get it" until you hear it said many different ways many times over. You especially don't get it until you begin to *live* it; that is, experience a thought concept as your personal reality. As a loving observer of human behavior, perhaps I can provide some fresh perspectives and novel directions, and maybe divulge a few feline secrets along the way.

✋ Karen:

This book is our gift—Connery's and mine, with the aid of many of my animal teachers—to help people recover their inborn connection with Nature and Spirit via the love they share with their animal companions, those magnificent creatures we call "pets." Such an inadequate word for the complex emotional bond we develop with the animal friends who share our homes and whose lives are so entwined with ours.

My personal background consists of years of fairly mundane living growing up in a Midwestern college town, attending a Big 12 school and getting my B.A. in English. My vague game plan for life was to get married so my husband could support me while I wrote the Great American Novel. Instead I married a man who is a gifted journalist and author. So I ended up supporting *him* while *he* wrote. No hard feelings; he's a far more disciplined and productive writer than I. Three months after graduating from the university, I was hired by the library there. What I blithely thought would be a short-term job turned into 28 years, most of them spent as supervisor of the serials reading room. Though I felt I wasn't really exercising my best talents, it was satisfying enough work. And working at a public service desk and supervising student employees, I certainly learned more about human nature than I ever had while earning a minor in psychology.

All my life, I'd enjoyed reading about people gifted with intuition and especially those who could telepathically speak with animals. I truly believed it was possible, but only for those born "wired" for these amazing abilities. I didn't really have a dream for myself, because I never dreamt someone like me could ever have the potential to access these wonder-filled realms.

Well, folks, the teachers with whom I've been blessed, both human and animal, have spent the past 14 years of my life proving me wrong. I'm here to tell you we *all* have the innate capacity for telepathic connection if only we choose to remember and cultivate it.

During my last few years at the library, I began using my accumulated vacation time to take training in psychological/spiritual and holistic healing. I kept having the nagging suspicion there just had to be more to life. My journey began as a search for my own healing, to find peace within myself.

Sometimes clichés are the truth and this one held for me: When the student is ready, the teacher will appear. What at the time seemed like random events led me to attend a weekend workshop in something called breathwork, facilitated by a woman named Linda Star Wolf. Years later, I told Star Wolf about my first impressions of her and made her rock with laughter. More than two dozen workshop participants had been hanging out all day, stuck in a Boy Scout lodge buried in snow after the previous day's blizzard, waiting for our facilitator to get a flight out of Chicago. The afternoon was wearing on when the tedium was broken by shouts of enthusiasm. Star Wolf had arrived! My jaundiced view was, Who the hell is this woman that we had to wait all day for her, anyway? Then she came striding in, trailing flowy garments, with a scarf wrapped Native American fashion around her forehead over her long blond hair. I remember thinking disgustedly, "Typical, hippy-dippy, California-type chickie."

By the end of that workshop, I wanted to throw myself at her feet and say, "Please! Teach me!"

That snowy weekend in rural Iowa was my invitation to see the world with new eyes and an expanded awareness. The start of a challenging, rewarding, frustrating, *incredible* opening in my life.

These days, my husband is taking his turn working the day job so I can be self-employed as a full-time animal communicator, shamanic arts practitioner, teacher, and writer. I'm a graduate of Star Wolf's Venus Rising Institute for the Shamanic Healing Arts (*www.shamanicbreathwork.org*), and am a Shamanic Minister, ordained through that organization. I'm a Reiki Master (Reiki being a form of energy healing) and I'm certified in crystal healing (utilizing the vibrational properties of stones to facilitate emotional and physical health) by TAOMCHI, The Association of Melody Crystal Healing Instructors (Melody being the author of the celebrated *Love is in the Earth* books). Please don't call me "New Age"—that term carries far too much baggage. You may call me "healy/feely" if you need a label. And if you'd predicted all this to me 20 years ago, I would have laughed in your face.

As Connery indicated, I've waffled for years over the writing of this book. The conflict lies partly in what I've learned along the way. For many years, I tried to do things on my own, reading so many books on metaphysical topics and studying hard, but ultimately I discovered that you need a spiritual community to support you. You really can't do it by yourself. That's why we humans have churches, synagogues, mosques, temples, sanctuaries…sacred spaces where we can gather. ("That's why you have animal companions," Connery adds.)

I find myself writing not that great novel, after all, but nonfiction that might seem like wildest fiction to some. My prayer is that this book may share with you some of my personal revelations and insights, even though these are experiences of the heart that words seem inadequate to convey. I'd like to offer you what my teachers have given me: the inspiration to instill a sense of wonder in your life, to give you permission and encouragement to look beyond the mundane. To learn to see and hear with your heart.

Heart Talk

"The lie is that it has to be hard."
~ the spirit of all Crows

1 ~ Fence-Sitters

🐾 Connery:

While contemplating the approach to our collaborative effort, Karen asked me, "Exactly who is our target audience?" I replied, "The fence-sitters." This book is fondly dedicated to the fence-sitters of humanity, my favorite people. These are folks who are not exactly doubters; they truly want to believe, but would desperately like to have some tangible proof of the Divine, just to be on the safe side.

Karen jokes that she has calluses on her behind from sitting on fences for so long. For years, I'd attempted to help her as one of her spirit guides (those discarnate beings who serve as loving support and counselors from the Other Side), but found it difficult to get her attention long enough to get much of a message across to her. Her fear, skepticism, and self-doubt kept her skipping away at the first hint of a spiritual missive. Confiding in a friend, she once described her first experiences of consciously opening to the Divine thusly:

"I worked up enough courage to ring Spirit's doorbell, but when I'd hear the footsteps coming to the door, I'd chicken out and hide in the bushes. Then I worked up to the next level, where I could make myself stand on the step as the door opened, but my eyes were squeezed shut, my fingers were in my ears, and I was singing LA LA LA LA at the top of my lungs."

Obviously, we guides had our work cut out for us. Then with the passing of Karen and her husband David's one remaining elderly cat, Karen realized she couldn't do without feline energy in her life. She put out a call to the universe for her dream kitten, a green-eyed gray tiger, and, having spent many a lifetime in feline form, I jumped at the chance to incarnate in order to work with her. I'm much harder to ignore when I can sit on top of her in the middle of the night, purring and patting her face ("and snagging my hair with your claws," adds Karen).

My entry into physical being helped Karen ease down from the fence onto the side of the believers. In those days, she was working for the university library and was acquainted with many of her coworkers. One of these acquaintances was married to a USDA veterinarian. She mentioned to Karen that country dwellers often tried to get him to adopt kittens from them. So Karen let the lady know that she was searching for the aforementioned gray tiger kitten, just in case her husband encountered one in the line of duty. The opportunity for a little miraculous maneuvering was set in motion!

Two days later, Karen arrived at her service desk and found a note advising her to phone so-and-so at the Royal Hanneford. She puzzled over what is a Royal Hanneford as she sorted the daily newspaper mail. Then—one of those marvelous synchronicities, the kind that demonstrate you're on the right track, sprang out at her. Most of the front page of the Altoona, Iowa, newspaper was covered with photos of trapeze artists, performing horses and elephants, with an article announcing the arrival of the Royal Hanneford Circus to be playing in town for the summer.

Karen was paying attention now. She immediately phoned her coworker to ask for details. She was told the USDA vet-husband had gone to certify the circus animals and in the course of his inspection, noticed several cats who belonged to the owners. They mentioned to him that one of their cats was pregnant and they were concerned about finding worthy homes for her kittens in an unfamiliar town. He noted that the mother-to-be was a green-eyed gray tiger cat and duly informed his wife who passed the information along to Karen.

Do you see how smoothly events unfold when all are paying attention and playing their roles? I now stoop to a base pun and say things were purring along…an accurate description of the energetic vibrations when everything falls perfectly into place. I now turn the story over to Karen.

✍ Karen:

We habitual fence-sitters really need only pay attention, follow the clues, and throw away the word "coincidence." Replace it with "synchronicity" and you can feel the electric thrill when you *just know* some little event that might seem insignificant to others is, in fact, a message…a heads-up from the Universe. Then the miracles can unfold. As a recovering skeptic, I now completely trust that, far from "seeing is believing," you have to believe it in order to see it. If you deny the possibilities, the energy is blocked and nothing very interesting happens. My favorite Albert Einstein quotation is, "There are two ways to live your life. One is as though nothing is a miracle. The other is as though everything is a miracle." I've tried it from both perspectives and heartily endorse the latter.

When I got the phone call that "Pretty Face" had delivered four kittens, I made plans to drive down to Altoona to visit. Connery and his siblings were a week old when I first met them. They were cuddled together inside a wire crate where their mother was confined to keep her from getting lost in the unfamiliar territory. The crate stood less than ten feet from the iron cage on wheels that housed the circus's resident tiger. Did I need any more evidence that these were the kittens for me? *Tiger*-cats!

How could these tiny little guys hold such huge lessons for me? The day I met them, I got to reach into their crate and I lifted the paw of the little brown tabby. His paw just covered my fingertip. When the time came to bring home our kittens, David and I were still deliberating over which ones to choose. My original thought was to adopt one of the boys and the only girl, but the problem was that I really didn't feel any connection with the female. So how to choose among the boys? We did the only sensible thing and brought home all three of them.

Next came our usual dance of what to name the new family members. David and I take naming seriously and there's always a spirited discussion before we can agree. The first to win his name was Brown Tiger who became "Jackie" after Jackie Chan. Jackie was the smallest but what a scrapper! David was sold on the name after watching the little guy attempt to leap to the top of the big cardboard box play fort, miss the jump, hit the side with a loud thud, and slide all the way to the floor, much like a Jackie Chan movie outtake.

Then the gray tiger who looked just like his mom, Pretty Face, won his name. He became "Misha," for Mikhail Baryshnikov, due to his ability to gracefully vault three feet into the air. The third kit was such a handsome little devil that we argued for days over what to call him. We agreed to name him after a good-looking, debonair actor, but couldn't settle on the right one. Cary Grant kept coming to mind, but somehow the name didn't fit. Finally I suggested Sean as in Connery, but David argued that sounded inappropriate for a cat. Out of frustration I said, "Then how about 'Connery'? Then we'll have a trio of international stars." Thus did Connery Craft come into being.

David and I had a blissful first week with our new babies (except for the fact that every night they knocked down or scaled the cardboard barricade we put up to keep them in their sunroom and out of our bedroom). I was so jealous the day David called me at work to tell me he was playing with them. He was chuckling as he told me the three kits were chasing each other around and around in a circle, on his lap. But by the second week, our world came crashing down; Jackie was becoming listless. Soon it was obvious the little one was very sick. The vets couldn't quite decide what the problem was and he spent the next week in and out of intensive care at two different hospitals.

I couldn't believe the emotional pain I felt over this tiny creature who'd been in our home for only a few days. I already loved him with my whole heart and not knowing how to help him was torment. The few evenings he was home between vet stays he spent curled in a ball on my chest. At first his jet-engine purr came back, but gradually that faded away as he again weakened. I put my whole self into sending him loving light and energy. Still, by Saturday afternoon he ended up back in intensive care and I was in misery.

Sunday morning, I took our huskies for a long hike along the river greenbelt near our home. The fall weather was glorious and it felt so good to get out with the girls in the crisp air. I had to concentrate on the dogs to keep from being pulled down the riverbank, so I was focused in the present moment and temporarily spared from my anxiety. When I got back, I told David happily, "This was the first time all week I've been able to get Jackie off my mind." And that's when the phone rang. Jackie had slipped away from his body only minutes earlier.

That was ten years ago and my tears are falling again. But what gifts Jackie brought me in our brief time together! It took me days to gather myself and weeks more to recognize my lessons. With the support of the local holistic community, I began to realize that Jackie had been in my life to teach me great compassion, not only for my clients who have been parted from their animal companions, but for my own parents. They lost their only son, my brother, to cancer several years before I was even born. My childhood was colored by a certain amount of resentment toward his family sainthood. Now I knew I was getting a mere taste of the anguish my parents endured as they sought treatment after treatment for him, only to watch him slip away. Jackie helped me forgive my father for his inability to truly reach out to me through the grief that crippled him the rest of his life.

Jackie also taught me that energy healing is real. He was able to stay in his body with my help. And the final lesson: That we humans have to understand when it's time to give our animals permission to leave. Jackie stayed until my attention was diverted by that dog walk, and when the energetic link was broken, he was finally free to cross over. I wish I'd made a conscious decision to release him, but he helped me understand the importance of allowing our loved ones to go when it's their time instead of begging them to stay for our own sakes.

Speaking of fence-sitting, I debated and debated whether to share Jackie's story here. Myself, I have mixed feelings about books about the human/animal bond that inevitably bring me to tears, but then I remembered that those tears are actually one of the gifts our furry kids (or hooved, feathered, or scaled) give us. We try so hard to stuff our emotions, but our animal companions force us to feel them. They crack our hearts wide open when they leave the physical plane, but that only gives our hearts room to expand.

I've learned that our animal friends can somehow pull the cosmic strings, so to speak, making sure they meet up with exactly the right humans. So many times, I've witnessed a beloved animal that has crossed over bringing the perfect successor to the grieving family. The shocking number of abandoned and unwanted animals in the world proves the process is not always successful, but the loving connection is magical when it does occur.

Our personal current example is our floofy-coated mostly-black husky cross named Natasha. David calls her The Feathery One for her long, plumy fur. Three months before Natasha came to live with us, our giant sweetheart of an Alaskan husky, Tundra, suffered a series of massive seizures. It was sudden and heartbreaking…after all, our boy was only nine years old. He spent the night in intensive care and when we went to see him early the next day, he was frightened and agitated, and unable to stand. I don't think he even recognized us. David and I knew it was time to release him.

Tundra left his body with David's tears falling over his face and my tears on his furry butt as we gave him one last "Mom and Dad sandwich." I was comforted by a vision of our late, great husky, Keeva, playfully pouncing on him as he ran joyfully to the Other Side. Still, the shock of his passing left me crying for days. As I sobbed the day after he departed, I heard his sweet little voice (always so incongruous with the long, tall 110-pound body he'd worn). Plaintively he said, "Mom, I wish you didn't have to cry so much!" In spite of myself, I smiled and replied, "Tundra, if I didn't cry, my head would explode."

Tundra's passing (following our beloved husky Angel's transition by only a month) brought The Craft Pack down to a mere two huskies. David and I would find ourselves sniffling as we came in after clean-up duty—the dearth of poop in the backyard only reminded us of our losses. One morning, I was answering e-mails when I had a sudden thought that I should look on the Internet for husky rescue groups in the Midwest. I quickly found Adopt-a-Husky, an organization based in Illinois. I scrolled through the twenty or so thumbnail photos of huskies waiting to be re-homed. I clicked on a few and read the descriptions, which ran down a list of characteristics for each, such as "Housebroken" and "Crate trained." Every Sibe that caught my eye had a "no" in either the "Good w/dogs" or the "Good w/cats" category, or both. One spunky-looking girl even had "NO, NO, NO!" in the Good w/cats category. So much for that.

I scrolled to the next row of thumbnails and my heart jumped. The very last photo looked so much like a female version of Tundra I could barely believe it. I read her bio; it could have been describing our "T-Bear" instead of "Dasher," as she was then known. I was certain that Tundra had been whispering to my subconscious to look for that website at that specific time. Dasher had been listed only the day before I went web-surfing. To cut to the chase, less than a month later, my friend Robie and

I were on the road to a town north of Chicago to go get the girl, a trip that took a little over six hours each way. That's the sort of thing we animal lovers do because, like dogs, we think with our hearts.

Being nearly as shy as Tundra had been, Dasher took awhile to settle into the family. She never responded very well to her name, so we asked if she'd like to be called Tasha/Natasha instead. She said it would make her feel like a queen. So we celebrated her new life in her Forever Home with a new name.

Now Tasha dances with me just as Tundra used to do. She adores standing in the middle of the Mom and Dad sandwich, too. She's getting to the point that she's almost as pushy about worming her way in between us when we hug as was the T-Bear. She solicits affection nearly as persistently, though the paw she taps me with is a bit smaller and more gentle. She helps heal our hearts every day we see her smiling face and watch her bushy tail wave.

God bless our animal companions for helping us learn to trust our intuition and follow our spiritual guidance so we can get off that uncomfortable seat on the fence and *trust*.

🐾 Connery:

Before we move to the next topic, I'd like to acknowledge the woman I think of as the Queen of the Fence-Sitters, Oprah Winfrey. Yes, of course I know of Oprah. Her energy has a huge impact and I'd be aware of her even without Karen's appreciation of her. Lately she's focused her attention (and therefore, the attention of the world) on improving the lives of animals. We were thrilled when she supported Susan Marino and the Angel's Gate animal hospice, especially since Karen took her very first animal communication class there and has infinite respect for Susan.

I call Oprah a fence-sitter because when she addresses topics of spirituality, she (rightly) presents opposing as well as supporting views. There are still many who present themselves as visionaries, but their concepts are flawed because they come from a place of ego instead of one of compassion and service, a place of heart. Caution *is* called for.

Oprah (respectfully) grills her guests on topics such as reincarnation, voicing the questions that are on the minds of many. She stretches her foot down from the fence and dips a toe in the water, so to speak. When she follows her heart, she jumps in all the way. Then she approaches the next metaphysical fence and perches there, scrutinizing the view in all directions before making any commitments. Bringing the work of Eckhart Tolle to a wider audience has opened the doors to greater connection between humans and the rest of the animals, and I thank her for that. People can't begin to speak with us until they meet us where we live—in the present moment.

2 - The Original Internet

🐾 Connery:

Those of you who may enjoy this book and tell your friends about it will undoubtedly encounter the skeptics who snort and say, "Look at the size of a cat's brain. How can he possibly have the intelligence to contribute to a book?" By reply, I'd like to point out the size and bulk of your earliest computers compared with the relatively tiny, yet powerful, devices you now use. Further, I have wireless Internet capability. Telepathic connection, in other words.

Humans can be justifiably proud of their literary and artistic achievements, the greatest of which serve to uplift your entire species and thereby the world. Obviously, I don't pretend to be an arts and literature critic, but I know what I like and I like those works which raise the vibration of the viewer or the reader. Those works which stir passionate responses which then lead you to greater empathy and compassion for *all* your fellow beings. And especially, I like stuff that just plain makes you joyously laugh out loud.

Your computer Internet is like the metaphor for, and the summary of, all the best and worst impulses of humanity in one massive network. While much useful information is transmitted across the globe, the serious flaw is that the Internet can also spread fear and deceit like plagues. Along with the forthright communication, it is frequently used to disseminate deliberate misinformation, political propaganda, and personal agendas. In other words, it can all too easily be used to perpetuate fear. And fear often begets righteous anger and violence.

The Original Internet, on the other hand, is telepathic communication between animals (human animals, too), which includes the emotions of the being sending the transmission. It's a lot easier to see/feel yourself as a part of All That Is when you're connecting with one another with the energy of the heart rather than an electronic network. We "critters" (as Karen lovingly call us) would greatly appreciate having the human race rejoin us in the telepathic ranks so you can know on a gut level that what befalls one affects all.

✋ Karen:

Animal communicators, or "pet psychics" (as they are sometimes called), are not the only people who can converse with animals. Everyone is born with the innate capacity for telepathic communication. My personal theory is that the telepathic ability fades as toddlers learn to speak. It's so much easier to avoid feeling the emotions of other beings when using the spoken and written word, while with telepathy you get the whole package. To echo Connery's statement, our animal friends would desperately like us to rediscover telepathic connection because it fosters compassion and empathy when you experience all the feelings of others and realize the bottom line: We really *are* all One.

🐾 Connery:

We live in a world of energy, and the sooner people come to understand that, the better off we'll all be. My hope and prayer for my human friends is that you may all one day become aware of the energetic net that connects all life. To be able to see or at least feel the dance of the energies between yourselves. (I suggest you again watch *The Empire Strikes Back* and pay special attention to the words of Master Yoda instructing Luke Skywalker—now there's a teacher who knows what he's talking about!)

Then you could know when there is an energetic imbalance between beings, an unfair, unreciprocated depletion of one's personal energy by another. To my mind, you use your monetary system as the primary physical symbol of these energy flows. Perhaps if you could perceive energy more directly, money would be of less importance to you. Fear and worry cause the energy to contract while joyful connection leads to expansion and flow, as illustrated by your stock market.

✋ Karen:

At this time, I usually don't see auras, the energy fields surrounding all living things. My dear friend Star Wolf is one of those people able to view people's energy fields and it's a capacity that the animals all share. A cat once gave me a mental picture of what a human being looks like to a feline: a glowing, shifting cloud of colors. The physical body is discerned almost as an afterthought. Once in a great while, I see a flash of aura. I was walking with two coworkers from the parking lot to the library early one dreary gray winter morning. Coming toward us on the sidewalk was an older faculty member I'd seen around campus before. When I first noticed him, he was about 100 feet away and I had the impression he was wearing a skull cap in bright parakeet green and yellow. But as he came closer, the top of his head was a brilliant cobalt blue. I was trying not to stare as I puzzled over why on earth he'd dyed his hair like a refugee from Cirque du Soleil. After he passed us on the sidewalk, I turned around and watched the blue glow still visible above the upturned collar of his overcoat.

"Did you see the color of that guy's hair?" I whispered to my friends. They looked around, confused, and both said, "No." I kept quiet after that, wondering what was wrong with them that they hadn't spotted the obvious. It wasn't until I got to my cubicle and brought up the screen on my computer that the truth hit me. The luminous blue screen reminded me of the color I'd seen on the man's head and with a jolt I realized I'd been seeing his energy field. I haven't a clue why I saw the energy that particular time, or why it was that intense blue (maybe he was in deep meditation as he walked?), except that I wasn't trying to make it happen. Forcing the perception never works…you have to *allow* it.

The same is true of reclaiming our innate telepathic abilities. Trying too hard just blocks the energy flow necessary for communication.

Telepathic Animal Communication

So exactly what is animal or interspecies communication? The very best definition I've ever heard was given to a close friend of mine by Amber, the resident donkey at Spring Farm CARES (Center Alternative Research Education Sanctuary, Inc.). Spring Farm is an animal sanctuary located in upstate New York and is known as the first public center for teaching animal communication. It's a place filled with angelic presence. I urge you to read their website at *www.springfarmcares.org* for the full story, or better still, go there and learn from human teacher Dawn Hayman and the master teachers in animal form who reside there.

Dawn had sent her students to wander around the farm and practice talking with the animals. My friend came across Amber in the barn and asked her, "Do you speak English?" The way he interpreted her response was, "I don't speak English, exactly. Or Swahili or Dutch or French or Chinese. I speak what you're speaking right now—which is the universal language of interspecies communication [telepathy]. It's almost like sound waves, vibrations, or impulses that humans and animals then translate into their own languages." She finished by telling him, "Look, I know this stuff seems absurd to you. But you just have to believe. That's why they call it 'faith.'"

I recognized the brilliance of Amber's explanation of how information flows in the form of energy between beings of different species. With telepathic communication, you listen with your heart instead of your ears.

My clients and my own students ask me how I receive information from the animals. It's a quick, subtle thing and can be easy to miss. I feel the emotions of the animal. Sometimes I see mind pictures like watching a movie screen; sometimes there's no picture and I only hear the movie's soundtrack instead. When the connection is particularly clear and strong, the energy automatically translates to words inside my mind and I can "hear" the animal speaking. The most difficult part is trusting that you're not just making it all up. Many times, I don't get an immediate validation for the information I've received and that makes it harder to trust. But just often enough to encourage me to keep practicing and perfecting, I get a message that is obviously correct to all involved.

While doing animal communication readings at a pet supply store grand opening, I got a very welcome reminder of the reality of the telepathic connection. I'd been speaking with customer after customer all day. People lined up with animals in tow from 10:00 a.m. to 3:00 p.m., a few coming back later in the day and standing in line all over again to bring a different beloved animal companion to meet me. It had been the busiest grand opening I'd ever worked and I was about ready to keel over when a man, two women, and three children approached my table. One of the women set a small black mutt on the tabletop and proceeded to explain that she and her family were considering adopting "Corky." They explained that the second woman was from the local animal shelter. I took a deep breath and said, "OK, what would you like to ask Corky?" The mom said, "Well, we want to know if we should adopt him." The dog, who had been wandering around the table, idly sniffing my signs and business cards, immediately swung around and marched straight toward me. He looked me right in the eye and I heard him say, "Tell them…to take me…*home*." He spoke slowly and with great emphasis, as though to an inattentive kindergartner. I repressed a chuckle, and just shrugged and said, "He says you should take him home."

Instantly, Corky was transformed into a delighted, dancing, wagging display of canine exuberance, frantically licking my face. We all laughed out loud as he dashed from one child to another, kissing each of them. It was as plain to the family as it was to me that I'd gotten his message loud and clear. Now *that's* the Original Internet at work.

Heart Talk

"I'm in awe of you. You're like a little kitten that I have to alternately bully and lick your fur smooth. Fearless, yet helpless. Let's explore consciousness together."

~ Connery, Karen's cat companion

3 ~ Wings for the Journey

"I am enough of an artist to draw freely upon my imagination. Imagination is more important than knowledge. Knowledge is limited. Imagination encircles the world."
~Albert Einstein

Connery tells me people tend to make an artificial distinction between what's "real" and what's "imagined." As children, so many of us got a pat on the head along with the condescending words, "My, what an imagination you have!" We learned early on to devalue our daydreams and flights of fancy. If we're lucky, we have a grown-up in our life who encourages our creative mental powers. Do you remember the scene in the original *Miracle on 34th Street* movie where Kris Kringle teaches the infinitely pragmatic little girl, Susan Walker, how to loosen up and pretend to be a monkey? I had to wait about 40 years for someone to teach me the importance of imagination.

My first breathwork retreat with Star Wolf was an amazing, eye-opening, life-changing experience. I told everyone who would listen with so much as half an ear all about it, always ending by saying, "It was the most incredible weekend of my life. But I'll never do it again." Ah, the famous last words. "Never" turned out to be about two years. I needed to learn some things during that time before I realized I was ready to attempt another breathwork.

Breathwork is powered by connected breathing; that is, one deep breath and forceful exhalation following another without pause. The breather lies comfortably on the floor on top of soft blankets and pillows, with a partner nearby to watch over and keep the journeyer safe during the process. Loud, rhythmic instrumental music, carefully selected to help move energy through the body, assists the breath in taking you into an altered state of consciousness. Following the breathwork session, the journeyer is taken to a table arrayed with art supplies. The next step is drawing or painting a mandala, a "snapshot" of the journey. The group later spends a great deal of time discussing the mandalas and the journeys they represent.

I came to that snowbound retreat at the Boy Scout lodge as a complete skeptic. When I laid myself down to breathe, I remember thinking, "OK, I want this to be completely real, not my imagination." With my eyes closed in the darkened room and above the volume of the instrumental music, I could hear sounds of powerful human emotions all around me. Crying, laughter, even pent-up rage released as shouts and screams. But I was determined to have a "real" experience and basically lay there like a rock. In spite of myself, I drifted into an awareness of being in a warm, dark cave. I could see a small, steady light, the size and brightness of a candle flame, but still and unchanging. In my mind, I heard my own voice speak words of forgiveness for someone whose behavior I'd never been able to pardon before. In my heart, I felt the relief of letting go of blame. Despite the loudness of the music and the intermittent noise of the other breathers, my world was suddenly one of stillness and peace. The moment was brief, yet profound.

But the truly astonishing part of that retreat was witnessing Star Wolf guiding two psychologically wounded young women through the depths of their emotional horrors and on to personal breakthroughs. Their transformations were nothing short of miraculous in my eyes. And to my utter amazement, I was one of the participants who moved forward to assist in the process instead of shrinking back from the intense psychodrama unfolding in the center of our circle.

By the time I committed to the next breathwork retreat, I'd had some training in animal communication and had a new attitude toward "imagination." I was beginning to see it as a viable tool for self-discovery and exploring the sea of energy in which we all live. And in the two years since I'd worked with her before, Star Wolf had refined her own Shamanic Breathwork™ technique. She's publishing a book about Shamanic Breathwork™, so more detailed information about the process will be available to the public late in 2009.

No longer limited by demanding *reality* in my breathwork process, I had a vivid, exhilarating journey. Star Wolf's basic instruction was "breathe until you're surprised," so I lay on my back and did the deep connected breathing until I could have sworn there was a friendly wolf standing at my head. Soon other wolves began to appear all around me, dancing in place and impatient for me to travel with them. So in my altered awareness, I got up and took off with them. I found myself running through the air high above a Minnesota landscape in the midst of a pack of bounding, loping wolves. I looked down at the shining surface of the lake beneath us and asked them whether we could go down and run across the water. Instantly, we dropped down and went skimming over the surface. I could see glittering rainbow drops splashing up around their paws.

Such breathwork visions as these appear much like dreams to me, except they are self-directed and do not fade upon returning to normal consciousness. You retain all the emotion, the detail, and the insights as clearly as in any waking experience.

In addition to Shamanic Breathwork™, which was my first true experience of an altered state of consciousness as I ran with the Spirit Wolves, animal communication instructor and author Penelope Smith introduced me to a more traditional type of shamanic journeying. My dear friend Phoenix Rising Star, cofounder of the Sedona (Arizona) HeartWalk Center, helped me refine my journeying skills, proving to me that I could drop my awareness down and within simply by rhythmically shaking my own rattle near my ear. I'd assumed I'd need someone else to drum or rattle for me and it was a revelation to find I could do it all by myself in a pinch. When I have the time and space for in-depth shamanic journeying, my preference is to play a CD recording of drumming designed for the purpose. I can gain much insight this way, though it generally doesn't have the life-altering power of the breathwork technique.

Now that I'm teaching introductory animal communication classes, I feel sad when one of my students claims to have no imagination. I make every attempt to support these people the way all my teachers have encouraged and empowered me. It feels so fulfilling to pass along the same kind of help others have given me.

I notice that the healy/feely community prefers to avoid the baggage of the word "imagination." Now they call it "guided meditation" or "visualization," which I assume has a more adult ring to it. Whatever term you use, it's a way of manipulating energy. You've probably encountered this concept through the hoopla over "The Secret" or, better still, the books and CDs of Esther and Jerry Hicks.

If you think animals don't have an imagination, then you've never watched a cat walk past a piece of string lying on the floor. A quick double take, a crouch, then the mighty pounce. If you didn't see that innocuous string transform into a snake, then you have less imagination than a cat.

Medicine Cards

Beyond the obvious ways animals have helped us—as companions, as workers, as sustenance—they can teach us how to look within for guidance. Animals have been teachers of mankind for centuries and not only among indigenous peoples. I offer Aesop's Fables as an example of humans using animals to illustrate lessons.

There are many tools available to aid you on your journey of spiritual exploration, and one of my favorites is the vast array of divination cards available these days. I'm fond of Doreen Virtue's many oracle card decks, covering such themes as angels, fairies, and Ascended Masters, but of course my ultimate favorites are animal cards. Jamie Sams' *Medicine Cards: The Discovery of Power Through the Ways of Animals* has been in print for over 20 years now. This deck of simple yet evocative drawings and the accompanying book remain one of the most useful vehicles to introduce you to the teachings of the animal kingdom. "Medicine" here refers to spiritual power and energy.

I encountered the Medicine Cards at my very first breathwork retreat. As I've mentioned, I was supremely skeptical and approached the cards with a SHOW ME attitude. The facilitators told us that selecting a seemingly random card was actually a synchronistic event. We'd be guided to draw just the right card from the deck. I closed my eyes and concentrated, willing my card to be Wolf. Instead I got a blank card (which I later learned symbolizes Unlimited Potential), so I selected another and pulled wimpy Butterfly. Looking back at my disappointment, I have to smile. Of course, Butterfly and the promise of transformation it carries was precisely the perfect card for me. I just didn't realize then what a life-changing journey I was embarking on that day.

Draw one card a day or use the suggested card spreads from the book and devote some time to contemplating the messages. As I always implore my students, keep a journal and write down your insights or they tend to slip away. Being able to go back and reread your own thoughts is an important aid to your spiritual growth.

As an adjunct to playing with the Medicine Cards (as Beaver once told me during a breathwork, "Work is play and play is work"), I strongly recommend you read the books of Ted Andrews, especially *Animal-Speak: The Spiritual & Magical Powers of Creatures Great & Small*. This particular book doesn't specifically address telepathic communication with animals, but it opens your heart and mind to paying attention to the natural world around you. Anytime I have an unusual encounter with an animal or repeatedly see the same kind of animal in magazines or on TV, I run for my copy to look up the critter to see what messages are trying to break through my day-to-day busy-ness. *Animal-Speak* also introduces you to the concept of Power Animals, your spirit helpers in the form of animals.

Power Animals

Just as we all have at least two guardian angels watching over us (see the Resources list at the back of this book for suggested reading about angels), we have spirit animals guiding and protecting us. Some are with us our whole lifetime while others come and go as we need their specific talents. If you wonder who are your power animals, look around your home. Do you surround yourself with paintings or sculptures of particular animals? Do you feel a special affinity with a species? These are strong hints of your spiritual connection with your power animals. For example, wolf art and photographs hang on the wall of nearly every room in our home. Wolf—the pathfinder and teacher.

I recall a conversation I overheard between two of my power animals. I was nearing the completion of an extremely intense advanced training with Penelope Smith at Spring Farm CARES. A fierce migraine was keeping me awake late at night. I was pleading for help from God, the Spring Farm angels, *anybody* who could give me some relief from the pain and nausea. I became aware of Wolf (always with me) and Eagle (who drops by as needed) discussing my situation. Wolf said, "I'll put my paws on her shoulders and you grab the top of her head in your talons and flap. That should stretch her neck!" I quickly changed my mind about asking for help, thanked them, and said I'd deal with it myself. So I wandered from the dorm area to the shower and sauna room to visit my buddy, Dakota, a huge gray and white tiger cat with a rose-petal-pink nose. He and the other three cats in his family were being sheltered while their people changed households. The shower room was the only space available for them.

When I walked into the room, all the cats were asleep. In misery, I lay down on the floor on my left side. Behind me I heard the whump-thump as Dakota hopped down from his favorite napping place on top of the sauna onto a tabletop and then to the floor. I glanced over my shoulder and saw him walking toward my feet. With a rumbling purr, he began pacing next to me, caressing me with the tip of his tail. As he reached the small of my back, he firmly head-butted me. A brief pain exploded there as the tension I didn't even know was there released.

He continued up to my shoulders and head, around to the front, purring and lightly touching me with his tail. Suddenly, I had a vivid impression of a medicine man shaking a sacred rattle over my body in a healing ceremony. When Dakota reached my feet, he strolled away and calmly jumped on the table and back up to his perch. Feeling a little stunned, I lay still for a few minutes before it hit me that my pain had diminished and I was feeling relaxed. Yawning, I thanked my shaman-cat friend/ Power Animal in the flesh, and stumbled back to bed.

Heart Talk

"Your protection must be stronger than your fear."

~ *the spirit of Nortie, Karen's late cat companion*

Connery Wisdom

✋ Karen:

When the graduates of Venus Rising attend advanced trainings, we're expected to take turns delivering the morning ritual. This consists of bringing together sacred objects (items holding special meaning for you, such as small religious statues, crystals, flowers, and other representations of the natural world, etc.) to create a simple altar and sharing words of inspiration, usually read from a favorite text. Sometimes we use the Medicine Cards, or a deck of angel cards, to offer direction to the group.

I was signed up to do ritual the morning before a breathwork session. Sometimes during the advanced workshops, Star Wolf suggests a focus for our process rather than the usual protocol of journeying wherever you need to go for greater self-awareness. For this particular breathwork, she had asked us to use our journeys to discover our heart's desire, a subject that can be difficult…at least I know it is for me. Since it's become something of a tradition—when I'm at Isis Cove, the North Carolina retreat center of Venus Rising—for me to ask Connery to write the opening ritual for me, he provided the following words of encouragement to accompany Star Wolf's suggestion.

⁂ Connery's Breathwork Advice, Nov. 2005:

Humans have a way of finding excuses for not reaching out for the golden ring. The animals who love you and observe your ways find this both amusing and frustrating. When you're happy, we're happy—it's that simple.

You've been presented with a great opportunity here today. Dig deep for the buried treasure. If you have animal companions in your life, we'll help. If not, you have power animals just itching to be asked for their assistance. So ask! Use this journey time to define what it is you want—make that the biggest thing in your heart and mind so it towers and shines above all the obstacles you've created. If you can't see the prize, you'll only see the barriers in front of it.

Karen asks me, "But what about fear?"

Use fear as a tool, a warning system that alerts you to move with caution, but take care to define your fear and pinpoint its source, or it overwhelms and stuns you instead of sharpening your senses. Navigating through your fears makes the prize all the sweeter, does it not?

Another suggestion for you to contemplate: As you journey, ask your guides to help you recognize which burdens are truly yours to bear and which actually belong to others. How can they become strong if you take on their burdens? They become weak and you become weak under all that extra weight. Redistribute the load. And then perhaps examine your own burdens—could they be transmuted from lead weights to feather pillows? The choice is yours. (We cats would definitely choose the feather pillows, preferably placed in a sunny spot.)

- Connery Craft, a cat

Heart Talk

"Death is just another experience, not something to be dreaded. People drown everything out instead of experiencing it. By not savoring the moment, the taste of food, the feel of the grass. Drowning out with TV, drugs, loud music, reading. Dulling instead of experiencing life."

~ the spirit of all Rabbits

4 ~ Facing Fear

🐾 Connery:

I'd like to address the critical subject of fear. Humans have taken a simple, vital, survival mechanism and elevated it to an art form. You allow your lives to be twisted by anxieties, the vague fears that something—if not cataclysmic, at least nasty—is about to happen to you. That you have to be on the alert, on the defensive, at all times.

Sometimes you even take yourselves out of the very moment that should keep you most present and satisfied: when you're petting your animal companions. "Is that a cancerous lump I feel under the fur? Oh, my God!" Stroking us should be an exercise in bliss and comfort for both human and animal, not a manual exam! Not to suggest you remain oblivious to physical challenges in your animal friends, but set aside an examination and evaluation time separate from the mutual pleasure of caressing us and feeling our love and gratitude in return.

A few observations, then.

-   You jump from fear to anger because it carries a slightly higher vibration and gives you the illusion you're more in control of the situation.

-   Fear and anger should be viewed as warning signals, flashing lights to alert you to a situation needing your attention; allowing them to be constant presences in your life is dangerous to your energy level and a drain on all those who love you, especially your children and your animal companions.

-   Anger is a response to fear; fear triggers anger—what is the fear that underlies your anger? Recognize the source of the fear to disperse the anger.

-   Fears left unexamined and unaddressed become chronic anxieties; better to look them in the eye and know your enemy.

-   Unexamined anger becomes an excuse to abuse others.

-   Ask yourself, when does preparation become paranoia? Perhaps the moment you begin to obsess over the dreaded event?

-   Worry is chronic, low-level fear, like an annoying hum from a faulty light fixture.

Now that I've asked you to consider these ideas, I offer the finest antidote to fear: GRATITUDE. To focus on every single thing for which you're grateful each day, from the titanic to the most miniscule. Karen jokes that when she has a bad day, the most she can come up with for her gratitude list is, "I turned on the hot water tap and hot water actually came out." It's a start, anyway.

My philosophy is this: I choose to see the whole instead of the holes.

Connery on Instinctual Fear Responses

Humans are far more instinctual than they'd like to believe. You have the same drives as the rest of the animals and you'd be better off just admitting it to yourselves right off the bat. It would be far less stressful than pretending you're "above all that."

Karen is now thinking about a video she once saw on the evening news. The film intercut clips of the body language of young men and women meeting in a bar with footage of the courtship dance of cranes. The attempts to attract and impress the opposite sex in human and crane were strikingly similar. Yes, a fine example of my point.

And believe it or not, we companion animals strive to overcome some of our instincts in our interactions with our humans. I try very hard not to lash out at Karen with my claws when she carries me past the dogs when it's their suppertime. In my mind, I know she's only acting for my own safety, but my instinct is to struggle and run away. I have to keep reminding myself of the very thing I'm always telling Karen: TRUST. I admit that fear is a difficult instinct to tame, but all of us can learn to deal more sensibly with this emotion. Harmony will follow.

Keeva Teaches Me About Fear

Karen:

Our second Siberian husky was Keeva, who grew from a tiny pup into a big, blue-eyed girl with a long, wooly gray coat. She was our great love and our equally great challenge. I spent her puppy-hood dragging one foot behind me like the mummy monster in an old B-movie because her teeth were habitually locked on my ankle. An obedience school dropout, she was so smart that she had me tricked into thinking she was too dumb to learn anything. I finally caught on when I realized all I needed was the right incentive, which in extreme cases called for an M&M. What a character she was! David could make her dance with delight by singing his own version of "Sheila," the Tommy Roe hit from 1962, to her: *"Sweet little Keeva, you'll know her if you see her. Blue eyes and a bushy tail."*

Certainly the most gregarious husky we've ever had (though our current Sibe, Aspen, comes very close), she was everybody's favorite. Just when I'd almost broken her of jumping up on people, we were on a walk and met a friendly guy who was admiring Elke and "the Keeve."

He recognized Keeva's outgoing personality and patted his chest, inviting her to hug him. As she gleefully launched herself into his arms, she looked over her shoulder at me. I wasn't consciously doing animal communication at that time in my life, but she clearly said, "See? They *want* me to jump up on them!"

Though she lived to be nearly 16, saying goodbye to Keeva was a tough one. (Of course, *all* transitions are tough.) We celebrated her life and times and often shared a laughing reminiscence of her antics, but it took me more than a year to be able to think of her without feeling a pang.

I was attending a shamanic retreat facilitated by Phoenix Rising Star at the time. She'd sent the participants out for solitary nature hikes on the grounds of the SE Nebraska 4H Camp where we were staying for the weekend. Feeling serene, I began to contemplate the amazing Keeva. What a bizarre combination of loving and ornery she'd been! Instantly, I heard her sweet voice in my mind: "I brought *Coyote* Medicine into your life."

I stopped in my tracks and literally smacked my forehead. Of course she did! Her entire lifetime was overflowing with trickster energy, the irrepressible feistiness attributed to Coyote in Native American lore. (And boy! was Coyote Medicine ever prominent at that workshop—the night we arrived, the local coyotes were holding a convention, yipping and yodeling and making a huge racket right outside our cabin.) Keeva had the Coyote power of frustrating you nearly to tears one moment, then doubling you over with laughter the next, as you finally perceived what she was slyly teaching you. Even from the Other Side, that day, she got me one more time.

I walked along one of the many paths behind the cabins, Keeva's spirit frisking ahead of me. Her presence was so tangible I could almost see her with my physical eyes. She led me across a footbridge and we followed a twisting path through the woods. A deer bounded away as we approached and wild turkeys ran through the fallen leaves with a sound like rushing water. Though enthralled, I really thought I was paying close attention to my surroundings. It started to get closer to dinner, when we were supposed to meet at the main lodge, so I decided I better double back. But the landmarks I thought I should see were nowhere to be found.

Proud of myself for staying calm, I kept walking until I encountered a couple with a terrier on a leash. I decided it wouldn't hurt to ask the locals for my bearings. As they passed me, I called out, "Is this the way back to the 4H Camp?" They looked at each other, shrugged, and told me they didn't know.

OK, now I was getting nervous. I knew that the camp adjoined the 300-plus acre Schramm Park and I began to have visions of wandering for hours in the dark, with the massive embarrassment of having search parties out looking for me. I spotted a sign pointing to the fish hatchery and figured at worst, I could veer over there and then hike the mile back up the road to the camp. But I'd be plenty late for dinner and have everyone worrying about me. Believe me, experiencing humiliation is a huge fear of mine, and I don't like to cause a fuss over myself, either.

I stood still and tried to calm and center myself. I called out to Keeva, but her presence was no longer there and I felt a familiar irritation with her.

As dusk approached and I was verging on panic, I came across a wooden trail marker. Though it seemed a little ominous that it was numbered "13," I decided I was at least on a main path now. The next marker was 12, a very good sign! I sped up, counting down the wooden posts. When I came to the edge of the trees and saw the 4H basketball courts in front of me, I nearly dropped to my knees to kiss the ground. That's when I heard a chorus of riotous coyote laughter in my mind. And Keeva was joining in the mirth. I felt a fleeting moment of annoyance, then broke down laughing, too.

I reflected on all of this as I walked up the hill to the lodge. I was chuckling over the fear I'd felt, even though I was never in any real danger. It was merely the fear of appearing foolish (and partly because, by then, I *really* needed a bathroom). To point out how subjective fear can be, it turned out my friend and cabin-mate, Sharon, was only 100 yards behind me all the way back. *She* wasn't worried in the least.

As Connery has pointed out, I learned that day that "navigating through your fears makes the prize all the sweeter." My senses had been sharpened by fear. The mundane camp food tasted like the finest cuisine at that meal and I radiated gratitude and appreciation with every bite.

Horse Medicine

Horses have also been master teachers for me on the subject of fear, and especially the joy you feel when you stand up to your fear and watch it dissolve.

Many people who practice energy healing wear a medicine bag or pouch around the neck, a container for small sacred objects that hold great significance for their wearer. Mine is a two-inch suede leather bag made in Sedona, Arizona, and it was a gift from my sister, Mary. It has a chip of shell (representing Water) and a tiny Herkimer diamond quartz crystal (representing Earth) glued to the outside. The element of Air used to be symbolized on it by a small brown feather, but it quickly wore away. I tried replacing it with other feathers, but gave up after a few tries. My feeling is that Fire is represented by the life force which once animated the leather from which the bag is made. I wear this necklace when I do animal communication consultations and any form of healing work.

In shamanic company, asking what's carried in your medicine bag is as rude and personal a question as, "How much money do you make?" or "Do you color your hair?" Maybe more so, since it's a deeply spiritual matter. But because I wear mine when I do in-person consultations at expos and pet supply stores, I'm frequently asked, "What do you have in there, anyway?" I'm not really offended, I know folks are only curious and don't realize what they're asking about. So I'll share it with my readers, too.

I honestly don't remember what kinds of stone fragments are in my medicine bag, but they're appropriate for my own healing and protection. There's a tiny icon with the face of Jesus on one side and Mother Mary on the other. It was given to me by my animal communication mentor, Sharon Callahan. There's a small medallion of St. Francis in there, too, also from Sharon. To me, the most personal and significant elements carried in this bag are gifts from animals; one of these is a single strand from a horse's tail, wound around a little clay horse I made for the purpose. How I came to receive that precious fiber involved a lesson about fear and self-honor.

When I began learning animal communication, I got a couple of readings from local intuitives since I had trouble trusting my own gut feelings. Both told me I'm definitely supposed to be working with horses. Maybe they got it backwards, that horses are supposed to be working with *me*. On my second trip to Spring Farm, I made up my mind to spend time with the horses there to work through my uneasiness about being around them. I'd always adored them…when they were on the opposite side of a sturdy fence. Sharon Callahan assures me I have "vast past-life experience with horses," but in *this* lifetime, not so much.

During that class at Spring Farm, I met Beth, another woman who felt timid around horses and wanted to learn to feel more comfortable with them. We agreed to go together to the big meadow and visit the four horses pastured there during our next break. As we walked and talked, I realized Beth was even more nervous about going in with them than I was. We made our way through a series of gates and when we got to the last one, I was about to unlatch it when I noticed a shining silver horse hair caught in the wooden fencing. Part of me *really* wanted to keep that strand, but I made a quick assumption that Beth needed it more than I did. She'd wandered about 20 feet down along the fence, so I called to her and said, "Here's some Horse Medicine to help you with your fear!" and I pulled it free and held it out to her. Her eyes lit up as she thanked me. I smiled, but felt a little twinge.

While Beth stayed on the outside, I let myself through the gate so I could walk downhill to the trickling brook, fed by the spring for which the farm is named. The horses were grazing 100 yards away, so I sat down by the water and scanned for the diminutive frogs I'd noticed on a previous visit. Out of the corner of my eye, I noted the horses were wandering closer. The big silver gray Thoroughbred/Arabian gelding named TLC was approaching me, slowly but steadily. He stopped directly across the stream from me where I could fully appreciate the size of his front hoofs only a yard away. Leaning down, he drank with a quiet splashing. I heard him say, "How can you be afraid of me? See how delicate I am?" Though he looked gigantic from where I sat, I reached a hand toward his nose. He hesitated. My thought was that he was afraid of me, but then the truth hit me—he was being careful not to scare *me*. With great care, he nuzzled my fingers. "We're showing Beth how to do this," he told me.

A moment later, I looked up to see Beth had come through the gate and was standing near me. She told me TLC had sent her a message as he tickled my hand with his lips and whiskers: "See? *She's* not afraid of me."

Beth and I stood there, excitedly comparing notes. After a couple of minutes, I noticed the horses slipping closer to us. Beth didn't seem to be aware of what was happening until I gently pointed out to her that we were ringed in on all sides by TLC and the other two geldings, "Tutti," the huge gray Thoroughbred, and Meloudee, the Arabian; and Ember, the dapple Thoroughbred mare. I was overjoyed that all I felt was a thrill of love for these incredible teachers, no fear whatsoever. They circled us for only a few moments, then quietly moved away. Obviously, they were making sure they didn't push us to the point of nervousness. We thanked them profusely for working with us and reluctantly left to rejoin our class.

Back in Kigercat Hall, the setting for class discussions at Spring Farm, I found myself recording a message from TLC in the margin of my journal. I'd been thinking about the single horsehair again when he came into my mind. "You give your Medicine away too easily—that Medicine was meant for you. Own our gifts to you, don't give them away so easily. Recognize gifts meant for you. Ask whether it's yours and take it if it is." Stunned by the full impact of this information (yes, I have a tendency to feel unworthy), I shared TLC's communication with the others. Beth tried to give the horsehair back to me, but I refused. "No, I gave it to you," I told her. "This is my lesson to learn. If I'm meant to have it, there'll be a strand for me out there."

After lunch, I dashed back to the big pasture. Though I eagerly scanned the length of the fencing, I found no more horsehair. With a little sigh, I went through the gate and returned to my favorite spot by the stream. I leaned out over the still pool where I could usually find my frog friends, but not even they were around. Suddenly, my focus moved from searching the bottom up to the water's surface. A glint of sunlight caught my eye where it reflected off the silver strand floating there. *My* Horse Medicine, I knew! But I saw it was a short strand, not like the long flowing one I'd turned over to Beth. That's OK, I thought, this is what I deserve for giving the first one away.

I carefully picked up the end of the hair and pulled it out of the water. And pulled. In awe, I realized it *was* full length, but this one was appropriately shamanic in coloration: half silver and half black. The Light, the Dark—no difference, as Star Wolf would say when reminding us to let go of judgment.

As other students wandered into the pasture, we began discussing our varied experiences as we watched the horses grazing far down the hill. Suddenly, all four of them raised their heads and they spun around to face us. Simultaneously, they galloped up the slope, shoulder-to-shoulder, straight at us. Out of the corner of my eye, I saw people move back to the fence line, but I had time to make a conscious choice to stand my ground. I knew that if I could trust any horses on the planet, it would be those dwelling at Spring Farm. I faced them with my feet firmly planted and watched as they parted less than twenty feet in front of where I stood. They thundered by me, two on either side. They passed so close, I could feel the rush of air, and the vibration of their hoof beats filled my body. I sensed their pride in me for passing their test and felt exhilaration. And now I had my horsetail strand to wear in my medicine bag to remind me of this moment of fear conquered.

A year later, I attended a retreat in California sponsored by Sharon Callahan. I got to visit Sharon's home and meet the beautiful Lily, Sharon's cat companion who assists her in the making of her wonderful Anaflora flower essences, created specifically to aid animals. When I told Sharon all about being rewarded with the horsehair, Sharon reported that she'd just heard Lily snort with disgust, "Horsehair? Pffft! Take some of *my* fur!" So I had the greatest honor of combing a little tuft of fur from Lily's ruff. It's carefully wrapped in decorated rice paper and is tucked inside my bag. Sharon commented that Lily had never told anyone else to take her fur. Wearing this gift around my neck helps keep me connected with the animal teachers who've helped me find myself. When I hold my medicine bag in my hand, I feel infinite gratitude for my animal guides and that keeps fear at bay by reminding me I'm *never* really alone.

There's another animal's fur inside my Medicine bag, but I'll save that story for later.

Heart Talk

As I'm struggling to feel my connection with Connery, and struggling never works...only flowing works, he tells me to take out my "Trust" bowl. This is a small ceramic bowl, sandy tan on the outside and sky blue with a spiral in the clay on the inside. Made just for me by a dear friend, Shirley Orf, this bowl has my name on one side and the word Trust on the other. OK, Connery, what should I put in this bowl? "Why, Trust, of course," he replies. When I respond with a snort, he clarifies, "Well, what represents Trust for you? Put that symbol in there then, if you need a physical representation."

"Now you're distracting yourself looking for just the right symbol," he tells me as I go on a scavenger hunt for Trust; "Anything will do." So I find my special little piece of tumbled sky blue Ajoite stone and place it on the spiral inside the bowl. It makes a pleasant ringing sound when I swish it around. Connery says, "OK, let that be the sound of trust for you. Let that sound center your concentration so we can get to work."

~ Karen

5~ The Orange Cat Conspiracy

Did you know the orange cats have a secret agenda for their human companions?

My teachers, Dawn Hayman and Penelope Smith, introduced me to the notion that the orange cats of the world are in cahoots with one another. Dawn refers to this as The Orange Cat Club and Penelope names it The Orange Cat Contingent. I like to call the network The Orange Cat Conspiracy (or O.C.C.); conspiracy not in the sense of a lurking menace, but more the feel of a sly smile and a wink. Think Newman and Redford in *The Sting*.

Not every orange tabby I've met is an active participant in this conspiracy, but my estimate is that at least three of every four orangies I've personally encountered are members. Those who aren't seem to either have fear issues to overcome or are pursuing their own personal agendas. Dawn taught me the hallmarks of an O.C.C. member are the tendency to be christened with a human name, have a great sense of humor, a daredevil approach to life, a fascination with water, "and they all know Sherman." Sherman is Penelope's venerable long-haired orange tabby who happens to be the chairman of the network. (You can see photos of Chairman Sherman on the "Home and animal family" link on Penelope's website, *www.animaltalk.net*.) I once mentioned the O.C.C. to a friend whose cat, Phoenix, is obviously a charter member. Since she's an intuitive soul, I suggested she ask him whether he knows Sherman. She reported that when she asked him, Phoenix looked away from her, gave her the mental impression of a shrug, and said, "Sure. So what?" Dawn says the typical reaction of an orange cat to this question is: "*Everybody* knows Sherman."

While Dawn was telling our class about the O.C.C., I was thinking of a certain daredevil *gray* tiger cat with a human name, a sense of humor, and an affinity for water. When I asked her about this, Dawn explained that the Orange Cats can have honorary members. Aha! I later asked my animal communication mentor, Sharon Callahan, about my suspicions of Connery. Her perfect description of him was, "He's an orange cat in a gray suit." The light bulb came on. When I sent my call to the Universe to bring the perfect kitten into my life, I pictured my favorite kind of green-eyed, gray tiger cat; that's whom I was looking for, not an orange cat. Connery had to be born in a gray suit in order for me to find him. As he describes himself, he's an orange cat traveling incognito.

It was during this same class with Dawn, held in a small town in Missouri in April of 1999, that I had my very first detailed telepathic conversation with a cat. Dawn had brought photos of Spring Farm animals and encouraged us to practice connecting to these master teachers just by studying their images. I picked out the picture of a snoozy-looking orange cat, thinking this would be an easygoing subject. Wrong. The name written on the back of the photo was Sonya Pia. To my vast amazement, Sonya Pia then proceeded to convince me that telepathic connection with animals is utterly real.

To that point, I still wasn't sure I wasn't just making it all up. But then I felt Sonya's insistence that I speak with her. It was like having a cat pacing on the table as you try to write, rubbing against you, paw-pats, head-bonks. I began having difficulty concentrating on Dawn's lecture due to the vivid mental impression of a furry orange form pacing back and forth in front of my face. Finally, I wrote in my notebook: "Sonya, I *will* speak with you as soon as we break for lunch. Before I eat, I promise." I asked her if I should talk to her on the sundeck and I thought she said, *Yes, away from the others.* I felt her settle back to wait for me. As we broke for lunch, Dawn looked me in the eye and said, "Be sure you talk with Sonya Pia—she *really* wants to talk with you." I thought, "No kidding!"

As the rest of the students flocked to our potluck lunch, I decided to test my connection with Sonya Pia and teased her a little, just to see what would happen. So I thought about getting my food before I'd try to connect with her, contrary to my written promise. Her reaction was a definite *No!* So I again asked her if I should go out to the deck: *Yes. And be sure to bring your notebook.*

Outside, birdsong was everywhere. I paused to listen, and could feel Sonya listening along with me with true feline alertness. Then, abruptly, she shook off her instincts and became the teacher again. As I sat down, I was pondering whether I was cut out for a career as a professional animal communicator/healer. I didn't phrase a specific question in my mind but she picked up on my thoughts and answered them. She spoke to me so clearly, I found myself writing her exact words in my notebook.

Yes, you are a part of this work, more than you can even imagine at this point. Through Sonya, I suddenly received a great wave of love from the animals of Spring Farm. I felt their presence arrayed in a semicircle before me, beaming loving energy to me. I sensed, I *knew*, the magic of the place and was instantly moved to tears.

At this point, I was so in awe I felt overwhelmed. Panic slipped in and my logical mind tried to make sense of it all: How am I supposed to do this? Oh, right, I ask questions. So I asked, "Sonya, are you Dawn's cat?" I immediately recognized this as a lame question, but it was all I could come up with in the moment. Her response felt vague and distracted to me, but I thought I heard, *We're all Dawn's friends, but I don't live with her* (information that was later confirmed). I had the sense she was mildly irritated by my trivial question interrupting as she was in the midst of imparting her crucial messages. Suddenly the connection snapped vividly back into place and I clearly heard her say, *Shhh. Focus!* I felt like a kindergartner. Then I began to think about my rudimentary training as a healer and wondered whether becoming attuned to Reiki should be the next step. *Learn Reiki and many other things,* came the response.

Come..Come..Come....To Spring Farm. I felt a longing to be there right now and began to fret over my limited funds for travel and training. Her emphatic words, *Trust! It will work out,* interrupted my thoughts. *So much to learn. We want to teach you. You have so much to teach, to tell,* the world.

*You **must** work with Dawn and Penelope. So much healing to be done.* I whined, "But I want to do my work in the Midwest, where I live." *Journey to learn, then you can bring it back to your home* was her reply. My mind had begun wandering again because she snapped me back to awareness: *Focus! I'm not finished.*

Reach out where you are. Place doesn't matter. I felt her warm smile: *Connect with orange cats......Listen!* The breeze came up and I heard it rustle the nearby trees. *Yes, keep listening to the winds. To nature.* I sat listening to the myriad birds singing all around and felt Sonya Pia had finished her lesson. Though it wasn't a physical sensation, I had the distinct impression Sonya was gently patting my cheek with her paw and telling me I'd gotten it well. Exhilaration swept through me and I wrote my feelings in my notebook: "Thank you, Sonya! Thank you from my soul!"

Still in tears, I was too choked up to speak, so I handed my notebook to Dawn and managed to croak out the question, "Did I get this right?" Dawn read over my notes and said, "You got it, all right." She then proceeded to bring me back down to earth by telling me that Sonya Pia was the Spring Farm recruiter. "So she tells this to everyone?" I thought a little mournfully. But still, I'd heard it all, *felt* it all, so clearly that I was proud of myself. And Sonya Pia had told me I had potential! I wanted her to be proud of me, too. Therefore, I always say I was called to my authentic vocation by an orange cat: Sonya Pia, the Head Barn Cat of Spring Farm.

An amusing aside to this story: When I told friends and university coworkers about Sonya Pia's message, I encountered the expected disbelief, but not always in the way I'd imagined. People were scoffing not at the idea I'd communicated with a cat, but that I'd communicated with a cat who was nearly a thousand miles away. Go figure.

The orangies can be a challenging lot. Their attitude is that humans are far too serious for their own good, so it's up to them to lighten things up. To me, they carry energy similar to those famous tricksters of Native American lore, Coyote and Raven. They understand that the quickest way to raise one's vibration is through laughter, so they'll do their damnedest to be comical for our benefit. O.C.C. members are irrepressible.

Chairman Sherman would like to chime in with another way the O.C.C.

helps people. He says, "Cats are solar batteries and we orange cats are particularly suited for this. We soak up the living vitality of sunlight and rub it off on our favorite humans. When we rub and purr against you, we're distributing showers of healing sun-warmth to the places of dark, congested energy in your bodies." And I know that Connery likes to deliver acupressure treatments when I'm in bed. He stands with all his weight on a tender, stuck acupuncture point until I can't tolerate it. My acupuncturist friend, Valerie, has taught me which of my energy meridians tend to harbor my sorest spots; Connery especially likes to apply pressure to the liver meridian points located on my outer thighs. *Ouch*, to say the very least.

At the moment, I have Connery locked out of the office because he was pestering me unmercifully for his late evening snack. He'll stand in front of the computer monitor, and when I shoo him away, he goes to the bulletin board and paws and chews at the Post-it notes or else gnaws the horn of the carved wooden rhinoceros on the desk. Through the closed door, I asked him, What else do orange cats have to say? His response was, "They like to be fed on time."

Heart Talk

Reflections on aging: "Time to be philosophical and reflect."

~ Tiger, a very elderly orange cat at Spring Farm CARES

"Life is still interesting whether you're on your feet or flat on your back."

~ Poppy Jay, retired racehorse at Spring Farm CARES

"You can still have fun even when you're an old fart."

~ Bogey, a black cat at Spring Farm CARES

6 ~ Resistance Is Foolish

The Orange Cat Council speaks:

Although our preferred method is to work subtly and behind the scenes via The Orange Cat Conspiracy, we would now like to issue a proclamation. This doesn't happen often, so kindly sit up and pay attention. This is our message for the human race:

RESISTANCE IS FOOLISH!

And what do we mean by "resistance"? We refer to the many varied and sometimes ingenious ways you find to waste or dissipate your life energy while attempting to drown out the voice of your inner knowing. For "resistance" you may substitute words such as procrastination, indecision, fearfulness; anything that describes how you put off living life to the fullest extent. This is the resistance of dragging your feet with every step, thinking, "What if this? What if that?" It takes less of your energy to make a decision and carry it through than you waste worrying about it and putting it off and attempting to avoid the situation.

And the most foolish resistance of all? The attempt to disown your feelings or hide them from others. You're not fooling anyone, you know. Certainly not your animal companions! We can literally see the energy you expend trying to hold *that* inflated beach ball below the surface.

Resisting experiencing an emotion, resisting being in the moment...all is energy tossed away. As our distinguished colleague Connery likes to say, "It's energy down a rat hole."

We model a different mode of being, we orange cats. We show you how to be in the moment, fully in your body. Watch us and we'll teach you how to live your life on the cutting edge of awareness, alert and ready for action when necessary and completely, utterly relaxed when it's time for rest. Perfect timing, perfect responses; no second-guessing. *Feel* your emotions, but don't get stuck in them; move through the full range. Do what feels good and right to you and *Lighten the heck up!* You are far too serious, so we do our best to make you laugh. The world needs you to be Light and laughing. Loving life and loving each other and knowing we're all in this together. Quite literally.

Thank you for your consideration of our lessons.

Karen:

I first learned of The Orange Cat Council during a meditation. An impression of a raised stage or dais occupied by a row of orange tabbies formed in my mind....I'd found myself called before the Orange Cat Council. Out of about a dozen cats, I recognized Sherman, plus others who had already crossed over, including my beloved recruiter, Sonya Pia. I stifled a laugh when I realized one of the members was that epitome of orange-cattitude, Morris. The situation reminded me of the scene in *The Sound of Music* where the nuns discuss solving a problem like Maria: Sonya Pia was asking the council, "How do we solve her *focus* problem!" Following some muttered discussion unintelligible to me, dear Sherman spoke up in his nonchalant way and said, "I'll endow her with my green laser vision." Bless you, Sherman, but I'm still not positive I've adequately activated your gift or how to use it. But I'm still working at it.

Once again, I came out of a meditation shaking my head in wonder at my own imagination. The Orange Cat Council? Right. As synchronicity would have it, it was only a few days later that my copy of Kate Solisti-Mattelon's book, *Conversations With Cat*, arrived in the mail. Her comment that she had posed her questions to The Cat Council was the first thing I read upon opening the book. Instantly I felt the truth: The Orange Cat Council is real and a subsidiary of The Cat Council. And I'd been the topic of one of their discussions? I experienced an odd mixture of feeling both embarrassed and honored at the same time.

I heard another message from the council one night as I was wrestling with whether or not to get going on writing *The Cosmic Purr*. Chairman Sherman, speaking on the council's behalf, informed me that not only was it all right for me to reveal the orange cats' agenda now, but Connery and I had been selected as the team to transmit the information to humans. The pressure was on!

Myself, I have a little familiarity with resistance. My co-author Connery may have mentioned this, once or twice. OK, actually he says I could be the poster child for resisting higher guidance. For example, one of the first things you learn about in animal communication or any intuitive training is the foods and substances that interfere with receiving the information; alcohol is often described as the worst culprit. Any foods that lower your energetic vibration are on the list to avoid, notably (oh, no!) chocolate. Back in my days at the university library, I had a student employee who enjoyed hitting post-holiday candy sales and bringing to work vast bowls brimming with little foil-and-paper-wrapped chocolates for all her coworkers. I would furtively grab a handful every time I went past on the way to my office. As I sat at my desk one day, cramming the treats into my mouth, Connery popped into my mind with a message: "You eat chocolate to resist your higher vibration." Such indignity; to be busted by my own cat, but I laughed, anyway. (If you'd like useful information about foods that enhance intuitive work and which foods detract from it, author Doreen Virtue has extensively covered the topic.)

Along the path to self-discovery, you find many helpful tools and philosophies. A friend sent David a book about the Enneagram, a model for understanding human behavior. The Enneagram posits that everyone fits one of nine personality types with additional complex shadings of combinations. I picked up the book one day out of curiosity. By the time I'd read the description of the fifth personality type, I was becoming more skeptical. By the time I got to the eighth, I was thinking this concept was similar to the substance that farmers spread on fields around here in spring. Then I read number nine, and, damn! there I was. To paraphrase, the Number Nine person can't make a decision to save her life and, once *forced* to make a decision, spends the rest of eternity wondering whether it was the right one. On the positive side, we Nines make great mediators and counselors because we can see all sides of a situation. I later discovered that many of my spiritual teachers and colleagues are also Nines, including a mentor of mine who describes herself as a "recovering Nine." The Orange Cat Council—and Connery—tell me they're very pleased that I've overcome my "nined-ness" enough to write their book.

As I devoted more time and thought to writing *The Cosmic Purr*, I found myself opening to deeper levels of communication with animals. As a professional communicator, my usual approach is to gain my connection to the animal via the loving heart connection of the human caretaker. I reach out to the companion animal ("pet") by first linking to the guardian ("the owner"). More and more, I connect directly with the animals themselves.

When I took one of our huskies to a new vet for specialized heart tests, I was amused to find a handsome orange tabby lounging on the counter of the reception desk. I stroked him as I walked past and asked the receptionist for his name: "Cy." Mentally I said hello to Cy and took Aspen on down the corridor to the exam room. Fifteen minutes later, as I waited for the doctor to run the tests, the door opened a few inches wider. I was surprised that they were done so soon, but it wasn't Aspen and the vet returning, it was Cy who came strolling in.

I set my purse on the floor to make room for him on the chair next to me, but he walked under the chairs instead. What the heck, I'll see if I can hear what he has to say, I thought. As he sniffed my open purse, I heard his words in my mind and nearly fell off my chair. He casually told me, "I wanted to meet Sherman's Choice." He then began rummaging inside my purse with nose and paws and told me, "You can learn a lot about a person from her purse." I replied, "So you're learning I'm a slob?" Congenially, he responded, "No, you're eclectic." And with that he headed for the door. I asked him to stay and keep me company but he told me he had a busy schedule and needed to get back to his duties. I suspect he runs the whole place.

Judging from this encounter, the whole O.C.C. must be referring to me as Sherman's Choice. I felt like royalty as I sat there grinning. And Aspen was given a clean bill of health; a great day indeed.

Still, I recently found myself once again waffling over what value my experiences might hold for others. (I'm a Nine; I can't help it.) So the orange cats arranged another proof for me. A longtime acquaintance from the university days called me in desperation. Julie's orange cat, Moonshine, had been very deliberately marking outside her litter box. The more I tried to unravel Moonshine's message, the more she became frustrated with me. I ran through all the common causes and thought we had the solution, but Julie called me back a week later and said the problem was continuing. I was so resistant to hearing Moonshine's answer that I had to meditate on it overnight and asked Julie to call me back the next morning. What I finally began to comprehend by tuning in to Ms. Moonshine was that she was concerned about Julie's outlook on life and wanted her to read *The Cosmic Purr*. Meaning I had to **write** *The Cosmic Purr* so Julie could read it.

When I explained all this to her the next day, Julie admitted she'd been in a dark emotional state for a while now. This surprised me, as I'd always thought of her as one of the most upbeat and good-natured people I've ever met. I also got the strong impression that Connery and Moonshine were teaming Julie and me up, so she promised to be one of my representative Iowans who would preview this text for me to make sure the message stays accessible to my readers. I got an e-mail from her later telling me that Moonshine was back to using the litter box, and that Julie had received a bulletin from her as she drifted off to sleep: "ORANGE CATS RULE!"

Concerning my worry that my information might not "play in Peoria," I can now hear the words of advice given me by one of my Dalai Llamas, Raindance. Raindance was one of Penelope Smith's two llama companions when she lived in California. I had the privilege of attending a three-day weekend retreat for professional communicators at her home there. To be honest, I was in awe of the llamas and didn't think I'd be able to hear them. On the last day, I was walking past the llamas' fence and noticed Raindance was pacing me, trying to catch my eye. So I forced myself to sit down on a nearby bench and let my mind go quiet. He said, "You worry too much about what others might think of you."

No kidding, Raindance!

"You should be more like Penelope and dance your own dance. Let the chips fall where they may."

I chuckled and asked, "Did I hear you correctly: 'Let the chips fall where they may?'"

"Yes!" he responded. "After all, they make a lovely mosaic."

Although this advice came from another species, it is orange cat sentiment, through and through. Of course, Raindance and Sherman lived together there for years and no doubt shared many philosophies.

It was also during that retreat that I had the honor of meeting Sherman in person. I was staying in Penelope's yurt with other participants and got up early the first morning to go use the bathroom in the house. Dawn was barely lighting the sky as I walked back to the yurt, and up the path to meet me trotted Sherman with Penelope's Afghan hound, Buddha Boy, side by side. I sat on a stone step and they sat down on either side of me and we watched the sunrise together. I felt sublime peace and a deep sense of community with all life and nature, sitting between those two great souls on the top of a mountain, the Pacific Ocean shimmering in the distance. A transcendent moment I'll always treasure.

While I was participating in Penelope's retreat, Sherman and the orange cats gave me a great gift of self-discovery. One of the group activities was facilitated by an artist friend of Penelope's. She provided us with black paper and white pencils and gave us a guided meditation about drawing mandalas from our souls. I was excited because I'd tried this medium on my own, but it never came out well. Now I understood that I'd been using the wrong kind of paper and that's why the dramatic white contrast hadn't developed on the black background. My intention was to depict the face of my very first cat, Nortie, the special friend who'd seen me through my teen years and some of the most difficult times of my life. I sketched in her large eyes and long, thick coat with the white pencil. Next we were given colored pencils and told we could add color over the white. My cat's eyes became brilliant green. I realized the face was looking less like my beloved cat (whose eyes were golden) and more like Sherman. When the exercise was complete, we passed our drawings around the circle. I saw the expression on Penelope's face when she studied my cat portrait and knew that it was meant to stay with her. In some ways I didn't want to part with that drawing—it was my rediscovery of talents I'd neglected for so long. But knowing that it brought joy to someone else was a special validation for me and I gladly presented it to Penelope for her birthday.

❧ Connery:

Now then, would you like to become an honorary member of The Orange Cat Conspiracy? There aren't any rules or by-laws, but there are some definite guidelines to live by. Celebrate your life and live it with enthusiasm. Cultivate a healthy curiosity and a sense of adventure. Practice discernment, but drop all judgment, especially as to "good" emotions such as joy and love, and the "bad" emotions such as grief. Just experience them as they come and let them move through you. Without the full spectrum of feelings, you're stuck in one place and that's just boring. In fact, make an effort to replace thinking with feeling once in awhile, and that would be a relief to us, your animal companions. We have to tune out your busy, busy thoughts most of the time or we'd be exhausted.

Laugh at your animals' jokes (they do those goofy things intentionally, just to make you smile, you know). Laugh at your own jokes, too. Laugh right out loud.

Be present in the moment. You throw away so much of your life vitality/energy fretting over the past or worrying about the future. Petting or playing with your animal friends is a great technique for staying in the moment, by the way. Just a suggestion.

Acknowledge the God-spark in all living things and feel your own connection in the great network of Life. No matter how alone you sometimes feel, you never really are.

Purr loudly and often. OK, since humans don't have the physical capacity to produce a sustained purr, you'll have to rely on the purring symphonies of your feline friends. Amplify that vibration in your mind and feel it in your heart, in every cell of your body, until you're buzzing with energy to the point you can hardly keep still. But then you do, after all, have your own version of purring: making music and singing. You create instruments to produce so many varied vibrations in addition to those of your own vocal cords. If you want to know what it feels like to purr, learn to play the Australian didgeridoo. Now *there's* a consciousness-altering vibration. So put on a recording of your favorite rhythmic music, quietly at first, then gradually build up the volume. Any music that makes you feel good, whatever gets you out of your recliner and moving your entire body.

Dance the Orange Cat Dance: Leap and bound through the air, twist and stretch your spine and limbs. Sense life's energies and respond with exuberance. Feel the energy of Mother Earth and the Sun and dance in that energy between them. Be silly in your abandon. Put on the music that makes you feel the best and sing and dance along. You can always do this in the privacy of your own home so the unaware, judgmental nonmembers don't report you to the authorities.

Claim your space and your right to be.

Heart Talk

"Don't be afraid to start something that looks complicated. Begin, and the pattern will emerge."

~ a spider at Spring Farm CARES

Life Is Just a
Bowl of Cherries

🐾 Ruminations from Connery:

I tuned in this morning as Karen was taking a shower. The energy of running water opens the intuitive pathways, so I love to listen to her ideas while she's showering. Sure enough, she began an interesting train of thought, pondering the cliché, "Life is just a bowl of cherries." YES! What an excellent metaphor! Let's play with it.

Hand a bowl of perfectly ripened, firm, sweet cherries to different people, and what are the various reactions? Do you perceive the fruit or the pits within?

"Oh, THANK YOU! I love cherries!" and this person immediately savors a few, then carefully packs the rest away in the refrigerator to enjoy later.

"Oh, THANK YOU! I love cherries!" and eats the entire bowlful, then spends the rest of the day with stomach cramps.

The next one says, "Oh, yes, I love cherries, but I can't eat them because I might break a tooth on a pit." Or the one who exclaims, "Pits be damned! I'll eat those cherries, anyway."

"Cherries! They're so expensive. I'll allow myself to just eat one and save the rest for a special occasion."

"I don't deserve to have cherries. They must be intended for somebody else."

"OK, thanks. But it's really not enough. I should have your cherries, too."

And then we have the person who will say, "Cherries? No thanks, I prefer strawberries," and walks away. Or the one who says, "Cherries? Actually, I prefer strawberries, so I'm going to go find someone with strawberries who likes cherries so we can trade." (Now, *there's* an equitable exchange of energy.)

Some eat the cherries and toss away the pits. Another eats the cherries and notices the pits might make pretty beads for a necklace. And still another eats the cherries and plants the pits to grow more cherry trees.

No "right" or "wrong" responses here, merely examples of how many ways the same situation may be perceived according to one's approach to life.·

Heart Talk

"Come be part of the family!"
~ a hen at Spring Farm CARES

7 ~ Snow Angel and the Raccoons

Growing up in Ames, Iowa, home of Iowa State University, meant looking forward to the annual VEISHEA parade each spring. VEISHEA being an acronym for the original academic disciplines at I.S.U., the student-run festival began as a showcase for the university to attract new students and celebrate achievements in education. University departments set up proud open house displays of their educational offerings, and service clubs operated food stands selling hotdogs and cotton candy. The festivities always culminated in the Saturday morning parade. When I was a kid in the late '50s and '60s, the frat houses would each construct an ingenious float in keeping with the theme for the year, sort of like the Rose Parade of academia. Marching bands traveled from all over the state to participate, clowns bounced along the route tossing candy, and university honchos and the state governor rode in open convertibles to wave to the crowds. Various student organizations entered smaller units in the parade and these were dispersed between the bigger floats for still more variety. It was during the VEISHEA parade when I was about 10 years old that I fell in love with Siberian huskies.

That was the year the student club from Veterinary Medicine participated in the parade with a team of five huskies in a single-file hitch pulling a guy in a two-wheeled rig. The dogs looked deliriously happy as they ran past the slower moving floats and marching bands, making their way down the parade route. Just a brief glimpse and they were past me. Then fate intervened as a large float got stuck navigating the sharp turn around Lake Laverne. Everything ground to a halt as organizers figured out how to resolve the hang-up. That is, everything but those huskies. Just as the waiting crowd was getting restless, the team came zipping back up the route, weaving in and out around the stalled floats. Cheers went up as they dashed by, entertaining the bored troops. I was enthralled.

When our elderly family dog crossed over not long after this, I of course pushed for a Siberian husky puppy. Mother, thinking of all that shedding hair, said, "No, you really want a Miniature Schnauzer," which was of course *her* choice. My husky longings went unfulfilled for many years, until I married David and we could eventually afford to move into our very own home. A home with a large fenced backyard. Perfect for a dog, I was sure, and I knew exactly what breed of dog.

David had been a self-described cat-sap since he'd left home for college and been adopted by a couple of kittens. When we moved into our house, our two exotic-looking silver gray Korat cats came with us. Neither David nor the cats felt the need for a dog in the family, but I was absolutely certain there was a dog-man latent in my husband. We'd lived there only a couple of months before I wore him down; as a result, Elke the pretty black and white husky pup came to live with us.

Raising Elke proved to be an education for both of us. David quickly reached the limits of his tolerance for shredded carpets and gnawed-on furniture. "She goes or I go," became his mantra. I was pretty damn frustrated with my dream dog, too, but we agreed to give her a last chance and enrolled us all in a basic obedience class. The instructors gave me plenty of useful advice to replace my rosy dreams of effortless dog-ownership. Elke graduated with the perhaps not-so-coveted "Most Improved Dog" award. David and I compared notes after filling out the questionnaire on the last day of school and discovered we'd both written down "This class saved our marriage."

By this point, the feud between dog and David had calmed down a bit. Then on our ninth wedding anniversary, we encountered one of those life-changing upsets as David was permanently laid off from the local newspaper where he'd worked as a writer. After soul-searching and discussion, we agreed that he'd try free-lance writing rather than look for another job. Instead of being left alone with the cats all day, Elke found that Dad was at the computer in the home office most of the time. She began to shyly slip into the room and under the kneehole of the desk, to curl up at David's feet. Gradually, he noticed how much she liked it when he rubbed her back and legs with his bare feet. Then he discovered that it nicely broke up his day to take her for long walks. I realized that the dog-man had awakened when I observed that David no longer rushed to the sink to wash his hands every time he'd petted Elke.

Some advice for those who think it'd be fun to adopt a husky: These dogs are happiest when they live with another husky. (Also, Mother was certainly right about the excessive shedding! I tell guests that's a felt factory on our living room rug.). We found this out when Elke began suffering anxiety-related illness around the age of four. I convinced David that getting another Sibe pup would give Elke companionship and playtime. Thus, Keeva arrived on the scene. And as Elke aged, and she no longer felt up to dealing with Keeva's energy and antics, you can guess my solution to that problem. This was my excuse to look for my new grail-dog, a blue-eyed white Siberian.

My quest for the white Sibe took place at a time I had no car of my own. Since David wasn't keen on adding a third dog to the family, he refused to drive me the 100 miles to check out a pup advertised in the Des Moines *Register*. Rashly, he said, "If you can find somebody to take you down there, you can get the puppy if you like her." By the end of that week, I was headed to Ottumwa with a friend and an empty cat crate just big enough to transport a 7-week-old husky.

Sibe pups who grow up to be blue-eyed have eyes the most amazing color of violet blue. I sat on the floor of the dog-breeder's house and looked into those violet eyes framed by fluffy white puppy fur. She was peeking shyly around a chair leg, sizing me up. When I clucked to her, her face lit up like the Fourth of July and she came scampering over to me. That pup had the most beautiful smile I'd ever seen on a dog, and it was a smile I'd see just about every day for nearly 14 years after that first meeting.

That little girl was a perfect angel all the way home. Forget the crate; she slept in my lap most of the trip. She'd been christened with her obvious new name before we'd driven 10 miles: the Snow Angel, Angel for short. A few miles outside Ames, we stopped so I could put Angel in the crate in order to safely introduce her to her new big sisters. And her new Dad, uh oh.

Two days later, I shamelessly eavesdropped on David as he told a friend about our new family member over the phone. "I saw them pull into the driveway and Karen got out without the puppy," he said. "I was so relieved! But then I saw her drag the crate out of the back and thought 'Damn it! She did get her.' I stepped out the door, ready to read Karen the riot act, but decided to at least look at the puppy first. Well, I took one look at her and went, 'I'm a dead man!'" From my perspective of their meeting, David came storming out of the house as I set the crate on the front step. Then he leaned over to look through the wire door and Angel's little tail began thumping wildly against the plastic crate. Angel was wriggling with delight as she looked up at David and I watched his face melt. It was mutual love at first sight.

From that first day on, Angel lived up to her name. Even crusty old Elke loved her and enjoyed playing with her, far more than she'd liked the aggressive Keeva. Keeva and Angel romped all over the yard together, Angel making little noises that sounded just like the high-pitched yips of fox kits. One evening, Angel coughed up a hairball, but it wasn't her own fur, it was Keeva's long gray strands. I had to laugh. When we'd take the three for a walk, little Angel would trot as fast as she could to keep up with her sisters, Angel always in the middle, looking up left and right at the big dogs to be sure she was doing it right.

Our adorable puppy grew into a beautiful, graceful, and good-natured dog who would ultimately teach me some of my most significant lessons as I practiced to become an animal communicator. I wrote about one of these for my website and have had countless people say, "Please thank Angel for me." Following is that story.

Angel taught me important truths about the reality of the world of Spirit. By the time she was seven years old, I was fully engaged in my spiritual/metaphysical studies and learning animal communication. Gradually, over a space of months, Angel's behavior had begun to change. She wanted to spend more and more of her time in our backyard instead of being with us in the house. David and I noticed that Angel would only come inside to bolt down her supper, then rush to the backdoor again. Normally, this was the dog who slept outside our bedroom door and rolled onto her back any time I had to get up to use the bathroom during the night. I always had to pay the "Tummy Toll," and scratch her belly on my way to and from the bathroom. We were puzzled that our friendly girl was shunning our company, although she'd greet us happily enough when we spent time with her outside. It got to the point that, one late afternoon, a drenching rain was falling in sheets over our yard and there stood sopping Angel, pathetically peering in the kitchen window, blinking the water out of her eyes. But when I went to the door to call her, she refused to move.

David's patience gave out, "You're supposed to be the animal communicator! Talk to her and find out what's going on." True, I'd taken just about every class available to train communicators, but I was nervous about putting myself to the test with Angel. I mumbled some excuse and turned away so I wouldn't have to see that forlorn husky face through the window.

A couple of nights later, I was in a peaceful mood and decided to make time for a deep meditation. As I settled in, I could feel the presence of my guardian angel, whom I think of as Sarah. I cast my thoughts east to Spring Farm, home of my Master Teachers, and connected with Sonya Pia, the orange cat who had recruited me as an animal communicator/ healer. As always, she didn't mince words, saying, "Why don't you talk with your own animals!" Well yes, there is the Snow Angel problem. So I turned my attention to her and said, "Why don't you want to come into the house, Angel?" Her immediate reply was, "I'm guarding the yard from raccoons." She let me feel a blast of her utter disgust for the brazen little marauders. But then, her telepathic voice dropped to a low mutter: "And I wish you'd quit inviting raccoon spirits into the house."

I reeled in surprise, but instantly knew what she was talking about. Long before I began opening to concepts that are now solid foundations of my understanding, I had a habit of blessing road-killed animals I'd pass on the highway. Then, when I requested a telephone consultation with communicator Susan Marino, the first thing she exclaimed was, "Wow! Your house is filled with animal spirits! Hundreds of them!" I'd pondered why our home would hold so many animal spirits when it hit me that they must be the spirits of all those poor road-kills. In her book, *Natural Healing for Dogs and Cats*, Diane Stein confirmed my suspicions. She cautions that when you bless road-kill, you need to be careful to ask the animal's spirit to go with the light or else it will follow you home.

And now, here was Angel dispelling any doubts I'd had about the existence of these spirits; I'd certainly blessed plenty of raccoons in past years.

Again feeling the presence of my angel, Sarah, I asked her to please gather up the raccoon spirits and any others troubling to our living animal family and take them into the light. I had a mental vision of her using a broom and literally sweeping every corner of our home. I saw a huge, fat raccoon sailing blissfully upward in a beam of white light. As she finished her task, I fortunately had the presence of mind to thank Sarah and I watched her recede into the light, a baby raccoon cradled in her arms.

Coming out of meditation, my first thought was, "Boy, do I have an imagination!" But what the heck, I'd go see how Angel was doing. When I opened the backdoor, Angel was dancing on the back step, wearing a huge grin. My jaw dropped as she trotted past me into the house. In the following days, David and I commented over and over how wonderful it was to have her back to her cheerful self. We hadn't fully realized how strange her behavior had become until she popped back to normal and we could appreciate the contrast.

Since then, I've been careful to rephrase my blessing spoken to the animals I see lying along roadsides. I now tell them, "You're out of your body. Go with the light and back to God, and blessings for your journey." Recently, David confided to me the blessing he gives them, and I was moved to tears. He tells their spirits, "Seek the light, little one, and go back to God if you haven't done so already. A big, warm, wrap-around hug of love to you on your journey. God bless your soul."

Angel's differences with the raccoon spirits serve as a good reminder that we need to cleanse our homes of negative energy on a regular basis. Until we deliberately clear them out, human emotions get stuck in the atmosphere of our living spaces. The energy of anger is particularly disturbing to our animal companions. Be aware that we let those energies into our homes every time we turn on a television or read a disturbing newspaper article. "Smudging" with sage smoke is extremely effective, but if you detest the smell of burning sage, there are alternatives such as using the ringing vibrations of Tibetan chimes to clear the energy. "New Age" book stores are a good source for purchasing smudging supplies and someone there will probably be able to tell you all about using them. These days I'm careful to warn my clients when I suggest saging their homes: one woman's upstairs neighbor called the police to report her for smoking pot after she smudged her apartment and she had to show them it was only sage she was burning.

There's a postscript to Angel's raccoon story. Our dearest girl has been on the Other Side a couple of years now. Two months after her passing, I was beginning to get over my grief enough to be able to hear her again. As I drove across the state to go work at a pet supply store grand opening, I suddenly felt Angel's presence riding shotgun with me. Thankfully, I've finally come to trust that these moments are real, so I just let myself enjoy her company. As I said my blessing to a dead raccoon, about the tenth dead raccoon I'd passed that day, I joked to Angel, "Do you help the raccoon spirits get to the right place?" Her reply was quick and tart, "Yes. I send them straight to Raccoon Recycling." Then she sent me a ridiculous mental image of herself garbed in a bright yellow HAZMAT suit. I laughed out loud. When I asked her the same question about a dead skunk we passed, she sent me an image of herself wearing a gas mask.

Any time I feel doubt start to creep into my spiritual life, I have only to remember Angel and the raccoon spirits.

A Journal Entry

My journals are filled with entries about friends pushing me to get going on this book, such as the one about my client-turned-friend, Elaine, who continually threatens to put on her "steel-toed velvet boots" to propel me into action. (I once jokingly hinted to her that carrots work better than sticks and with glee she replied, "That's a great idea. I'll hit you with a sack of carrots!") But I certainly never expected anyone to send me motivation from the Other Side.

I don't make deliberate attempts at mediumship. Several of my friends regularly receive messages from those who have crossed over, but I ask God to protect me from hearing humans since I'm dedicated to being a voice for the animals. I was mulling over my fears of becoming "too open" when the spirit of my cherished white husky, Snow Angel, came into my mind. She explained that she's my gatekeeper, like a spiritual appointment secretary (mental image of her with reading glasses propped on her muzzle), and she screens all those wishing to speak with me. She showed me I'm protected from negative or interfering energies by a team of what I think of as my Spiritual Bouncers—all my animals who've gone over, backed up by defending angels. So usually the only communication I get from "dead" people is when they convey a message via the spirit of an animal. Angel lets only a choice few human transmissions through. This entry in my ongoing journal chronicles one of these, an experience that still amazes me.

Friday, September 8, 2006:

These ponderings are so bizarre and feel so much like my ego running amuck that it's hard for me to put them down here. David and I (and at least half the rest of the world) have been so depressed this week over the freakish event that claimed Steve Irwin's life...I asked Connery for some insight into why this happened. I kept seeing his passing as a light winking out in the world, but Connery showed it to me as a bright light passing through the veil and continuing to shine from the other side. I've been seeing/feeling Steve's energy splitting into diamonds of light all across the Earth; now he can be everywhere at once. It's as though his boundless enthusiasm is now powering hope-filled ventures for the whole planet.

What's particularly weird for me is that I feel Connery or the Orange Cat Council or somebody has recruited Steve to be one of my butt-kickers for the writing of *The Cosmic Purr*. When I thought of Steve as a cheerleader for the project, he popped into my mind and quickly corrected me: COACH, not cheerleader! I was arguing that all this is purely my imagination (What the heck *is* imagination, anyway?), and said, "Why would Steve Irwin's spirit possibly care about this book?" He told me with tears in his eyes that I have to write it for his children, that it's one of the ways to raise the vibration of the world so it'll be a better place for them. For their future.

I haven't dared hint at any of these thoughts to David; it would be the last straw in his wife "taking the road less traveled." I've talked to Robie about it and maybe I'll run it by my buddy, Kathy, since we share our innermost metaphysical experiences with one another. I better check in with Connery, too. Of course!

OK, Connery says it wasn't the O.C.C. or he who recruited Steve, it was Angel. Makes sense...she's a very persuasive dog. The impression I'm getting is that Steve's spirit is pushing a number of projects that will aid in raising the consciousness of the planet. Scary, scary thought that this is one of the reasons for writing *The Purr*. Makes me feel the urgency. He tells me no one will even have to read it to help raise the vibration in the world, but that he'll make sure it *is* read.

(Boy, I sure hope I got *this* one right!)

Heart Talk

I spoke with Angel's spirit not long after her passing. She told me the physical challenges in her last two and a half years were to teach us both about vulnerability. "I was a tough old 'wolf,' and I needed to learn these lessons," she said.

When I began to fall back into self-doubt that I was truly hearing her, she was very patient and understanding. She laughed when I asked her if she could send me a sign—lots of hawks or a flock of soaring vultures or something. She teased me that I always need a sign.

I forgot all about the sign thing for an hour or so, until I walked into the Out-Stamping Designs store (my favorite supply source for my rubber stamp addiction). The very first thing that caught my eye was a bold text rubber stamp that read YOU DID GREAT. Instantly, I felt Angel's warmth and love surround me and I knew that was my sign.

~ Karen

8 ~ Shamanic Journeys

I must point out here that although my website is *www.animalshaman. com*, I don't consider myself to be a shaman. I chose that as the name for my site because of the collective energies that I can tap into that I think of as The Animal Shaman. You're not a shaman unless the people you serve honor you with that title, and it requires long years of training to reach that level of experience. When I asked him how to describe my credentials, Jerry Standing Bear White, my teacher who *is* an authentic shaman of the Western Cherokee Nation told me I can honestly refer to myself as a shaman-in-training. By my certifications through Star Wolf's Venus Rising organization, I'm a Shamanic Breathwork™ Master Practitioner and an ordained Shamanic Minister, but it would still be highly inappropriate to call myself a shaman. (Star Wolf jokes that she just calls herself a "shamanatrix.")

Though I've heard shamanism described as the world's oldest religion, I prefer to think of it as the perception of the wisdom of nature and the world of spirit—the recognition of the God-spark in all living things and in the Earth herself. Living within the spiral cycles of life, death, and rebirth, and understanding we must die to the old to move on to the new, just as the seasons cycle through a year. Star Wolf has taught me how to be a walker between the worlds of the mundane and the spiritual, to search inside myself to find healing and how to support others to find their own healer within. She has now taught me to move through the cycles of change with greater grace and acceptance, an amazing feat when you consider my Enneagram Nine personality.

For months stretching into years, I argued with myself over the viability of my dream vocation as an animal communicator and shamanic healing arts practitioner. Journeying eventually helped reinforce my determination to leave the stifling security of the day job. I recall one breathwork in particular that expanded my awareness and strengthened my spiritual bond with animals. The entire process was filled with lessons both from animals I personally know and from the over-souls of entire species. It was during this journey that the spirit of Beaver advised me to "Abandon the Puritan work ethic and adopt the Beaver work ethic: Work is play and play is work." In my mind, I heard so many animals encouraging me, teaching me, that I couldn't even identify everyone. My heart and my energy field were wide open.

It was in the midst of this beautiful sense of community that I felt Star Wolf kneeling by me. My conscious mind realized she was performing a soul retrieval for me, restoring a lost, inaccessible part of myself. As she blew the energy into my body, I felt a wave of joy. Later she told me how *she* had experienced my soul retrieval and I was stunned. She described seeing a snowbound, frozen lake surrounded by woods. Incongruous in the white scenery, she came upon a large green frog who told her he was the guardian of a piece of my soul and it was time for me to have it back. Frog hopped over to a hole in the ice and explained that it was hidden deep under the water.

Calling for allies, Wolf and Beaver arrived, and Star Wolf dove beneath the ice and found me as a teenager, tangled in seaweed and frozen in place. Beaver gnawed through the strands and Wolf pulled us all up out of the water. On shore, the animals came to my aid. Buffalo came and gave me his robe. Beaver brought wood and Snake rubbed around and around a stick to light a fire.

As she watched my face regain color and begin to thaw, Star Wolf looked around and, through the trees, saw animals gathering from every direction. For a moment, she was at a loss for words as she recounted the story; then she exclaimed, "It was like the whole zoo!" The animals told her they'd been keeping this piece of my soul safe for a very long time until I was ready to have it back to use it. It represents my instinctual love of life, and they told Star Wolf they'd protected it for me because I'm a spokesman for the animals and their survival depends on me, and people like me. (And yes, at the age in which I appeared in Star Wolf's vision, I'd been emotionally withdrawn and mildly suicidal.)

Star Wolf's shamanic story, combined with my own breathwork experience, was powerful motivation for me. Yet it took another couple of years and a private shamanic journey outside the breathwork retreat setting before I could totally commit to my authentic vocation. I no longer remember the circumstances surrounding this journey, only that I was sitting in the easy chair in our home office at the time. With my headphones reverberating the drumming CD, I visualized diving down through my usual entry place to the Lower World, an abandoned wolf den located beneath huge gray boulders in the wilderness near Ely, Minnesota. (Penelope Smith recommends using an opening in the earth that one personally knows.) In my vision, I soon found myself standing at the crest of a high, rounded hill. I could see and sense animals surrounding this hill on all sides, reminding me of Star Wolf's soul retrieval story. Vast plains and forests populated by hundreds of animals were in view, the sky was filled with soaring birds, and in the distance whales and dolphins breeched in sparkling ocean waves. I felt awe.

I turned to face my companion on this journey, a lithe black panther whom I recognized as the journey-self of my first cat, Nortie, long ago crossed over to the Other Side. I watched as she smoothly morphed from cat form into a golden-skinned goddess cloaked in velvet black. She stood before me and offered me an object I perceived as a short spear tipped in quartz crystal. Without pausing for thought, I reached to take it from her, but she drew back and I understood that this must be a deliberate decision. I hesitated for only a moment, then stretched out my left hand. She nodded once and passed the object to me, which I then realized was not a spear, but a sacred Talking Stick, the symbolic tool giving one the right to hold the floor and speak without interference. I understood I'd just made my life commitment to speak for the animals. As I triumphantly held my talking stick high above my head, a roar rose up from the animals all around. I'd finally made my choice.

This background in shamanic journeying was later to serve me in good stead, aiding our own dog, Skyler.

9 ~ Skyler's Shadow

Our husky-mix boy, Skyler, came to live with us because Tundra spotted him out our front picture window. Tundra was making such an excited, squeaking ruckus that I went to the living room to see what was going on. He was plastered against the window, watching a six-month-old husky trotting down the sidewalk all by himself. I went out and coaxed this handsome young man over to me and carried him to our fenced-in backyard, then called the cops on him. I assumed his owners would want him back and he had no I.D. tag, so I thought it best to inform the local animal shelter. In the hour he was with us that day, I let Katie out to meet him and they had a great time playing together. David came home while the pup was still in the yard and noticed he was damp, so he immediately grabbed a dog towel warm from the dryer and went out to rub the rain off his fur. I watched as he looked up at David with loving gratitude. Then the van arrived. I could have kicked myself when I saw the desperate, pleading look in his eyes as the animal control guy dragged him down our driveway.

Long and involved story short, I kept in touch with the shelter and even went to visit the boy. They turned him loose in the exercise yard with me. Though he was busy exploring the fence perimeter, as soon as I sat on the ground and called to him, he came galloping to me and threw himself into my arms. Of course, I was in love. When the former owner finally decided to relinquish him weeks later, he came to live with us. David christened him Skyler, which means "shelter," pointing out that I could call him by the more healy/feely sounding name, Sky.

By the time I got to bring him home, Skyler was much bigger than the pup I'd easily carried to the backyard. Tundra was less than pleased about Sky's masculinity, too, so I quickly made the appointment for his neutering surgery. I stupidly didn't think to explain to him that he'd be at the clinic overnight, but I'd be back to get him.

When I arrived to pick him up, I anticipated a happy greeting from him. Instead, the vet tech had to restrain him as he frantically searched for the nearest escape route. He looked like a trapped wolf. I felt terrible for letting him think he was being abandoned again and I called out to reassure him. His head whipped around, he spotted me and froze in his tracks. Infinite relief filled his eyes and the poor guy stood there and whizzed all over the floor in an extravagant demonstration of submissive urination, the canine equivalent of "Thank God! You're here!"

Exceeding our vet's estimate of his ultimate size, Sky grew to be a gorgeous 80-pound dog with a thick coat colored pale gray and beige, with beautiful eyes of a luminous light golden brown. From his appearance, my best guess is he's half Siberian Husky and half Alaskan Malamute, so he's either our Alaskan Husky (the catch-all name for husky crosses) or our Siberian Malamute. At first he proved to be a bit of a challenge as he turned out to be a Houdini-husky. We thought our five-foot-high chain link fence was pretty secure. After all, it had managed to keep four Siberians and the gigantic Tundra in the yard for years. But not Skyler. He scaled the fence like Spiderman up a wall. After we installed wire overhangs on the top of the fence, thwarting his mountaineering tendencies, he began excavating instead. We folded heavy wire mesh fencing lengthwise at a 90-degree angle and attached it to the bottom of the chain link. The folded fencing extending into the yard curbed the tunneling, but we've always had to check the perimeters for spots he'd weakened enough to squirm under. The times he managed to get out, all he did was run around the neighboring yards for a while, and then try to get back in. It must be the challenge that appeals to him, or the memory of being stuck at the animal shelter.

All in all, he was a pretty well adjusted guy considering how many times he'd been picked up by animal control before we got him (thankfully, we always quickly got him back inside when he escaped *our* yard). His only problems were a bad attitude toward dogs outside our family, shyness around other people, and the blind panics he'd go into on dog walks any time he spotted a van the size of the ones used by animal control. He once pulled me off my feet because of workmen standing near their truck. After a tetanus shot and a week of changing the gauze over my road-rash, I devoted a lot of time to healing his terror of vans. It took him years to believe me when I promised that I would never again call someone to haul him away. Our animals are such perfect mirrors for us: Sky reminds me to work on my own abandonment and betrayal issues, some still unresolved from past lives, I suspect.

Skyler was a contented, couch-spud of a house-husky for his first year with us. He made me laugh out loud one day. He was sprawled out on the loveseat, head and right front leg draped over the armrest. As I walked past him, he opened one eye, looked at me, and said, "This is one sweeet gig!" He was an appreciative, cuddly boy with both David and me, radiating love with every bit of attention we gave him. Angel even complained to me that Skyler was always boasting to the other dogs about how much we loved him. Then, quite suddenly, he began to exhibit alarming behavior. Occasionally, we'd reach out to pet him and be met with a low, menacing growl. He began to snarl and snap at the other dogs, particularly Tundra. One evening when I was home alone with the fur-kids, he terrified me by attacking Tundra out in the yard. Thank God, T-Bear just turned his wooly shoulder towards Skyler and looked away. Had he reciprocated the aggression, there was no easy way I could have broken up a fight between two such big and powerful dogs. Sky chewed at Tundra's thick ruff for a minute, then his fury subsided and he was back to normal.

We could no longer trust Skyler to respond to us in a loving way. After he raked David's cheek with his teeth one evening, we began to fear euthanasia would be the ultimate solution for his erratic rages. David pointed out that you could see it suddenly come over him: Skyler's eyes would literally turn black just before the snarling began.

I consulted my animal communication mentor, Sharon Callahan. Sharon described the attacks as feeling almost like mild seizures to her.

She said Sky would get an uncomfortable, prickly, electrical feeling, then dissociate, leaving his body to run on pure instinctive defensiveness. She made a custom formula flower essence for him, which helped, though not enough for us to feel safe around him.

Eventually, I grew sufficiently desperate to attempt a shamanic healing for Skyler. Again, I dove down through the wolf den crack in the boulders into a dark forest setting. I didn't really know what I was looking for, but felt a calm determination. My journey animal guides were slipping between the trees on all sides of me. I noticed a narrow luminous trail like molten lava flowing along the forest floor and became aware that this was the track of the dark spirit that was plaguing Skyler. I strode along following the glowing ribbon, using my talking stick (which had elongated in my hand) as a staff.

Abruptly, the woods opened into a large, round clearing, and in the center a huge shadow beast reared on its hind legs. I perceived it as something primordial, shaped from dark smoke into a form that reminded me of the extinct giant ground sloths I'd seen depicted in books. But this shadow form sported six-inch claws and fangs, all glowing a smoldering yellow, as were its eyes. It appeared to roar, but there was no sound.

With foolish confidence, I raised my talking stick, which had now morphed into a long spear, and marched forward. Instantly, my four horse friends from Spring Farm burst from the woods behind me and galloped in a circle around the beast, preventing me from moving forward and also hemming it in. I suddenly realized that though this seemed to me to be a dream, I was in actual peril here. I fell back to assess the situation.

From four directions, my cats in journey-form appeared: Tiger Connery, Golden Lion Misha, Jaguar Jackie and Panther Nortie. As the shadow beast swatted at the milling horses, the cats crept closer and then sprang simultaneously to land on its back, each pinning one of its limbs to the earth. Now I understood what to do and calmly stepped up and plunged my spear between the shoulders of the shadow.

Instantly, a soundless explosion of white, orange and yellow laser rays burst from the point where my spear penetrated the shadow form. The shockwave sent the big cats and me flying through the air, rolling end over end, and when I picked myself up off the ground, I saw the beast was gone. To the side of the clearing, Skyler shakily stood with our other dogs nudging and licking him. I knelt in front of him and pulled wisps of remaining darkness from his eyes and nose and sent it to be transmuted in the Light. With a feeling of mission well accomplished, I returned to the mundane world.

Despite the previous success with Angel and the vanquishing of her raccoon spirit nemeses, I approached Skyler with caution. He did seem more stable. Over the next few days, we found that though he was still a little testy with Tundra, he was enjoying our attention. Eventually we realized we could trust him again—our sweetheart was back. Sharon Callahan checked his energy and pronounced him clear. She told me he was vowing to hunt my "shadow" for me in return for the help I'd given him. And his healing proved to me that work done in the altered state of a shamanic journey can effect vast energy shifts in the "real" world.

Months later, I was attending another breathwork retreat where one of the topics was protecting oneself from taking on others' "stuff." I remembered Sky's promise to track down any negative, shadowy energy attaching itself to me, and began to worry that he'd take it on himself and suffer a relapse. I asked him if he knew how to handle negative energy and he sent me a reassuring mental movie. I saw him shaking the tar out of something black and rubbery looking, then he dug a hole and dropped it in. Pushing the dirt with his nose, he covered it up and provided a final flourish by lifting his leg to the mound. I grinned and heaved a sigh of relief.

Heart Talk

"I dream of hunting rituals. I feel my tiger muscles, claws, and fangs as I bless my prey with my gratitude. Even if it's 'only' a mouse."

~ Connery, Karen's cat companion

10 ~ The Predator and the Prey

Katie the Shrew Hunter

In her book *Animal Voices*, journalist and author Dawn Baumann-Brunke introduced me to the idea that predators honor their prey with songs of prayer before the hunt. I remembered reading about Native Americans practicing the same sorts of rituals when I was a kid in school, and how I smugly thought of it then as a quaint superstition. How little we "modern" people perceive of the world!

Our blue-eyed white Siberian, Katie, taught me about these concepts in greater detail. Katie is the last of our "natural children"; in other words, she's the only remaining dog we purchased as a puppy. Everybody joining the family since Katie has been a rescue in need of a new home. David was the one who picked her out at the breeder's. The puppy I asked to see ignored us and ran wild. I thought we were going to have to make a flying tackle to catch her. Then David asked to see the little white one. When she was let out to play, she frolicked around the yard but kept coming back to us and going belly-up for tummy rubs.

After we played with the puppy for 15 minutes, the breeder put her back in the kennel and we retreated to the car to debate. Katie just sat patiently by the chain link, watching us. David took one more look at her and muttered, "Get out the checkbook." David had her named before we'd driven a mile toward home.

With our previous girls, we'd shared the training responsibilities in dog obedience classes, but David was the one who took her through Super-Puppy class. A favorite photo of mine is their graduation picture, with David holding Katie up in the air, both of them sporting a huge grin. So there's no surprise that one of her nicknames has always been Daddy's Little Princess. When David confessed to my animal communication mentor, Sharon Callahan, that although he's always careful to give all our animal companions equal attention, Katie is his favorite, Sharon said, "Oh, they all know that! Katie tells them all the time."

Sometimes the people closest to me will pick up a bit of information from an animal. Maybe they're a little more open because they know what I do for a living; I like to think it's my good influence. I was working in the kitchen late one afternoon when David came in from the daily backyard clean up. He had the dazed look I know so well. I've seen it on the faces of my fellow animal communication students and I've felt myself wear it many times. I knew he'd heard an unexpected message from somebody outside. He told me he'd found a dead shrew in the narrow run at the back of our dog yard and that he'd heard Katie boasting, "Yes, I'm the one who killed the shrew. As the hunter, I say a little prayer for them before I send them off to Valhalla." Then he said to me, "I made that up, right?" I replied, "In all the years I've known you, I've never heard you use the word 'Valhalla.'"

Fascinated by this information Katie had given him, I asked her if she'd teach me the prayer and she replied she'd be happy to do that. The cat mentioned in *Animal Voices* had learned the hunting songs from her mother, so I asked Katie if that's where she'd learned the shrew prayer. "No," she said, "I got it from the Wolf Council and it's really for hunting meadow mice, but it works fine for shrews." Then she recited it for me: "Oh, Shrew, exquisite expression of creation, give me your life force in exchange for my perfect love. And I return your spirit to God. Thank you."

Another excellent reminder of the need for constant gratitude. Katie's prayer helps me remember always to thank the plants and animals who sacrifice themselves to nourish me.

From The Rabbits' Point of View

From speaking to numerous groups and my own animal communication students, I know predation is a highly charged topic. I attempt to describe to them how a breathwork journey gave me the opportunity to understand the predator/prey relationship on an intimate level. During this particular journey, my consciousness rode piggyback with a wolf running down a rabbit. I experienced the kill as a loving, joyful energy exchange instead of an act of violence. The wolf was filled with gratitude toward the rabbit and the spirit of the rabbit was in turn honored to provide its body as sustenance for the wolf's pups. People have argued with me that a prey animal can't possibly feel love for the predator, but we're speaking of the soul level here.

I've conversed with the teeming rabbit population on the I.S.U. campus and the insights they gave me were remarkable. When I asked a bunny, "How old are you?" the reply was, "It doesn't matter. I'll be back many times." They comprehend that their place on the food chain is toward the bottom and it's no big deal; they understand that they'll return in a new form. The campus rabbits spoke to me of being fully alive in the moment: "Can't waste your energy worrying about the 'might be,' just be alert in the present. Feel us in our strength, the depth of our experiencing, nothing held back. Think of us to remind you to stay in the moment." As a group, they told me, "We feed the Mother [Earth] then spring back. We *are* the cycle, the breath of creation." They told me that they make Mother Earth's energy visible to us humans and invited me to dance the energy with them.

I always felt the campus rabbits formed one of my support teams when I still worked at the university. For years, as I wrestled with the doubt that I could be an effective animal communicator, they did their best to reassure me. As I drove to work at 7:00 one morning, I noticed a rabbit nibbling grass next to the curb on my daily route. About 20 feet up the street, there was another rabbit, sitting right at the curb. Then another! I glanced up the road and saw a rabbit stationed every 20 or so feet along the curbside. They weren't all lined up facing the road, but they were evenly spaced along my path. I pulled into the parking lot: more rabbits. I walked the three blocks to the library and there were rabbits scampering on the lawns. By the time I got to the backdoor, I'd counted 17 rabbits. Figuring I'd probably missed a few, I began to think of this as The 21-Bun Salute. When I had my conversation with the campus rabbits, I asked what the salute was all about. They told me, "That's just what it was. A tribute to you for listening to us. A signal that we know you. Do you know us? Thank you for acknowledging us." Remembering this experience, I feel very loved.

The Mouse Quandary

Loving respect is what is often missing in the human relationship with wild creatures. My personal challenge is with the mice that find a haven in our garage and attic. I used to live-trap them and drive them a mile away to a greenbelt area far from other houses. But I couldn't bring myself to release them in snowy wintertime, so I tried to ignore the fact that our ceilings were coming alive with mousy activity. And one spring day, as I opened the trap, I looked into the petrified face of the mouse I was letting go. When I had to shoo it out of the trap, I realized that by tearing it away from home and family and dumping it in a foreign environment, maybe I wasn't doing it such a favor after all.

Having mice cavorting in the garage and attic wouldn't bother me if not for the potential for electrical fires ignited by tiny teeth gnawing the wiring of the house. Seed for our wild bird friends and dog kibble are favorite targets, too, if thoughtlessly left unprotected. We once forgot to store a whole bag of the blue jays' peanuts in the shells inside a canister. In a few days, all that was left was an empty plastic bag and peanut shells in every nook and cranny of the garage. So I contacted the over-soul of mice. I apologized for what I must do, but I have my home and all within to protect. I asked the mice to relocate if possible, and warned them that if they stayed, I'd be setting traps for them. The mouse outlook, as far as I could determine, was that was a fair solution. Their lives are brief, anyway, they explained to me, and they rarely get any feelings of compassion or remorse from the humans in whose homes they've taken up shared residence. Being treated with respect would be a decent trade-off.

Though it breaks my heart, I use the traditional snap mousetraps in our garage. I feel it's the most swift and humane way of killing the mice, plus they have a decent chance at a bit of revenge as I've snapped my own fingers more than once or twice.

As I first began setting traps, I'd find many sprung with no mouse and the bait missing. An odd thought occurred to me and I decided to recite my own version of Katie's shrew hunting prayer as I baited and set the traps. And the traps began to fill up every night. At first, I was saving the tiny corpses for a friend with a snake-owning acquaintance, but David discovered the double-bagged bundle at the back of the freezer and that was the end of that. These days, the mouse bodies return to the earth inside our compost bin, and their spirits receive my gratitude and a reverent blessing.

Misha and Connery also have an interesting relationship with our house mice. Mr. C will spend patient hours crouched in the laundry room next to the garage, waiting for a mouse to answer his call. When he catches one, he carefully grabs it in his mouth and carries it away from the washer and dryer where escape is too easy. At first, he tried letting a mouse go in the living room, but Katie pounced on his prize and chewed it up. So he learned to run through the house, carrying his catch past the gate that keeps the dogs out of cat territory, namely our bedroom and the attached sunroom. There he turns it loose and he and his brother spend happy hours playing literal cat-and-mouse. David and I are less than thrilled with this practice. Many a night, we've had to try to sleep serenaded by scuffling and squeaking.

The first year that Connery began the mouse catch and release program, the cats never killed the mice. It was amazing to watch how careful they were with them. They'd pick up the mouse and carry it, but always let it go again. One afternoon, I saw Misha carrying what I was sure was a dead mouse and I let out an involuntary yell of dismay. Misha flinched and dropped the mouse, which promptly made a miraculous recovery and sprinted for cover behind a heavy bookcase. Another time, I looked for their living toy and found it sitting between pieces of furniture, calmly grooming cat-spit off its fur.

David and I always took pity on these mice and kept big plastic cups in the sunroom so we could scoop them up and let them go in the backyard. I noticed Connery staring into his water bowl one day, watching the mouse he'd dropped into it swimming frantic laps around and around the perimeter. I spoiled his fun by promptly fishing it out with a cup and releasing it outside. After they realized we were going to take away their mice, the cat boys began to kill them after giving them a sporting chance at escape under furniture or into a heat duct. Or maybe they just decided to save me the agony of indecision once I'd started snap-trapping mice. I really couldn't see the point in saving a mouse from the cats just so it could later be killed in a trap.

Connery and the Goldfish

Five years ago, I remembered that we had a perfectly good 10-gallon aquarium wasting away in the garage. While David was at work, I set it up in the kitchen and went to visit the pond fish in the backyard. I sent out a mental invitation to any baby goldfish who might want to come spend the winter inside and ended up with five little cuties who allowed themselves to be caught. But I'd hoped to catch the unusual bluish fish I'd been watching all summer. He was nowhere in sight, so I sent out a call to him and explained that I'd really enjoy having him come live in the house with us. After a moment, he appeared and swam toward me. It took a bit more convincing, but he finally came close enough for me to net him. Another triumph for animal communication! Anyone who has an ornamental fishpond can tell you how difficult it is to catch a specific, healthy fish without first draining most of the water.

At first, David grumbled about having a fish tank again, but then I began to notice he was spending time watching the fish and delighting in their enthusiastic response to him. Soon he insisted on taking over their feeding. Next he demanded that we get them a bigger aquarium. Nowadays, we have three remaining large, pretty goldfish (including the blue boy), spoiled rotten in a 30-gallon, filtered, aerated tank complete with expensive fake-rock landscaping.

When I first installed goldfish in the kitchen, the cats were understandably enthralled with their new Cat TV. They'd sit on the table opposite the aquarium, fascinated. We joked about "the food chain in action" when we saw one of the dogs intently watching a cat intently watching the fish. The aquarium's novelty wore off fairly quickly, though, when the cat boys discovered there was a hard cover protecting the fish. David's interest in them, however, only increased. He took to talking happy-talk to them and doing what he calls The Finny Dance in front of the tank. Whenever Connery heard his dad making a fool of himself over the goldfish, he'd run into the room, jump on the table and paw at David. "Dad, *please*! For God's sake, they're cat food! Pay attention to me instead," was his usual plea.

Connery was sitting in the dark kitchen late one evening, staring idly into the lighted tank. I decided to tease him and bent down to look at the goldfish who of course came running to greet me, wriggling with joy. I "tickled" them through the glass, turned to Connery and said,

"See? Aren't they sweet?" With a deadpan worthy of Morris himself, he looked me in the eye and replied, "I should think they'd be more salty than sweet."

Heart Talk

Sometimes, I sense Connery tuning in to me when I'm in the store buying cat treats. As I walked down the aisle, searching for the right section, I looked at the sign to my left: "Dry Cat Food." I looked to the right and read another sign: "Dry Cat Food." I glanced ahead to the end of the aisle and noticed an aquarium swarming with little goldfish. Connery's telepathic voice popped into my mind: "Wet Cat Food."

~ Karen

11 ~ Compassionate Connections

Misha the Healer Cat

Anyone who doubts whether animals are capable of compassion need only read the accounts published by Susan Chernak McElroy in her profoundly moving and inspiring series of books, beginning with *Animals as Teachers and Healers*. Not only do animals actively assist their human friends, but one another, as well. A handful of personal experiences of one animal's concern for another stand out in my memory.

When Connery and his twin brother, Misha, were less than a year old, our first husky was in her decline. Elke had developed some sort of neurological problem that caused her to walk with an odd gait and seemed to interfere with her depth perception. One night that winter, I let the dogs out for their late evening relief trip and went about getting ready for bed. Suddenly, I heard Elke howling from the backyard. Looking out the door, I realized she'd fallen into the deepest fishpond in our water garden. I rushed outside and found her thrashing in the icy water, shrieking in terror. Everyone who loves animals can guess I hesitated for barely a moment before sliding into the pond, thigh deep and wearing only my nightgown. I was so afraid for my dog that I really didn't notice the cold. I hoisted her onto the snowy yard and crawled out after her. The poor old dear was shaking so violently she could barely stay upright on her legs, so I carried her into the house.

I was frantic, fearing she would go into shock, and the only thing I could think to do for her was to put her in the bathtub and run heated water around her. David and I poured the warming water over her back for a few minutes, then he lifted her out and we toweled her off. Elke stood next to the tub with her head hanging nearly to the floor. She was still shaking uncontrollably and making a horrible wheezing sound. I honestly thought she was having a heart attack.

I recall that David and I stood back at this point to discuss what we should do next. In that moment, little gray tiger Misha came running into the bathroom. He calmly hopped up on the toilet lid, then onto the lavatory stand and ran to the far end, next to where Elke was drawing rasping breaths. We watched in awe as he leaned far over the edge until he could reach Elke with his left paw. His next action was so deliberate it left us no room for doubt. He patted her firmly between her shoulder blades three or four times, then pulled himself back up, turned around and trotted out the same way he'd come in. David and I exchanged a "Did you see that!" look. It was obvious to us both that Misha was sending healing energy into Elke's body as he touched her. Grabbing more dry towels, we rubbed her fur again and her struggle gradually eased. Soon she was able to walk on her own again.

I'll always marvel that Misha knew what to do when David and I were at a loss. I wasn't yet trained in Reiki healing at that time, so Misha stepped in and took care of Elke for me. Unlike Connery, I don't often hear word messages from Misha, but during a meditation a few years after this event, I heard him tell me loud and clear, "I'm your golden healer cat!" I can feel the healing energy pouring from his golden heart with every purr, every rub, and every kiss he gives me. God bless him! We're so grateful to have him in our lives.

Reminiscing about dear old Elke in turn reminds me of Angel's self–appointed role as Pack Manager. When Keeva would play too roughly with Elke, bumping shoulders with her and nearly knocking her off her feet, Angel would always intervene. Many times we watched Angel place herself between Elke and Keeva, then herd Keeva away and distract her attention from Elke. A year later, when the big Alaskan huskies, Tundra and Skyler, were part of The Craft Pack, Angel would referee as they playfully sparred. She'd follow them around the yard, barking her head off, if she felt they were getting too wild. I scolded her for barking late one night, warning her we could get in trouble if our neighbors complained about the noise. Her retort was, "Then talk to the boys!"

The Good Samaritan of Squirrels

When I was a kid, I remember how my great aunt pontificated about the superiority of man over animal. As the self-appointed matriarch of our family morals, standards, and practices, she stated that man was elevated above the animals by virtue of his ability to reason. Even then I had doubts about the validity of her hypothesis, just from observing the family cat. Were my aunt alive today, I wonder what she'd say to discount my next story.

My favorite streets are those where the tree branches reach to touch from one curbside to the other. I love walking or driving beneath these shady canopies. In my days of working at the university library, my usual route home included Burnett Avenue, a street lined with towering, mature walnut trees. My nickname for Burnett is "Squirrel Alley," and I always drive it with one foot poised over the brake pedal, alert for the walnuts being ferried back and forth.

One afternoon, I turned onto Squirrel Alley and slowly drove up the steep hill, watching out for the flashes of foxy-colored fur. At the crest of the hill, directly in the path of my car, I spotted two young adult squirrels in the street. I stopped eight feet from them and felt the usual pangs of sorrow for a little one crushed by a car. I began to recite my blessing for the one lying in the roadway, but was distracted by the behavior of the second squirrel. Paying no attention to my car, she braced her front paws against the limp squirrel's shoulders. To my utter amazement, I realized she was deliberately pushing the body toward the curb. Why would she care about moving a dead squirrel off the road? I wondered.

For a moment, I debated getting out of the car to help, but I couldn't take my eyes off the unfolding drama. I put on my emergency flashers; the least I could do was block the road for the little rescuer. She'd push her sister (for that was my impression of their gender and relationship) a foot or so, pause for a bit of rest, then push again. When the inert squirrel had been nudged across seven feet of pavement and was resting safely against the curb, I carefully drove around them and went home.

I felt dazed by what I'd witnessed and decided to try to tune in telepathically to the heroic squirrel. Immediately I heard a shout in my head, "Send Reiki!" I'd been saying prayers for the animal species struggling with the West Nile Virus that summer, so their Medicine Cards were right there on my home altar. I picked up the Squirrel card and held it in my hands, streaming Reiki energy through it to the one in need.

After a few minutes, my curiosity became irresistible. I replaced Squirrel on the altar and grabbed my car keys. Back at Squirrel Alley, I cruised up and down the street three times, looking for the "dead" one. But the only squirrel in sight was off in the distance, running past someone's house. Now a new picture was forming in my mind. The squirrel I assumed had been hit by a car had actually fallen from the overhanging branches onto the pavement and was knocked unconscious. Her sister gave her time to safely revive by moving her out of the traffic path.

No one, not even my late aunt, could ever convince me that squirrel was acting purely on instinct by pushing the other out of the way of cars on the street. Animals recognize the humans who connect with them at the telepathic level and I could sense the trust placed in me, the *knowing* that I would keep the road blocked from other cars. Still, that little squirrel never flinched or left her sister's side as I pulled up only a few feet away, and I was moved by her courageous determination. It was a privilege to be witness to this rescue and I was happy I could play a small role in it.

I have to wonder….How many miracles like this are happening all around us in the world of animals, every day? As we carry out our important human obligations, are we so oblivious to the animals' potential that we miss the wonders happening in our own yards? My personal experience leads me to think we write off far too much as coincidence or (that bane of scientific inquiry!) anthropomorphism.

Kayla's Story

Because animals can perceive human energy fields, they recognize animal communicators, also calm, sympathetic people, and energy healers. I got first-hand evidence of this while visiting the Cleveland

Metroparks Zoo on my first trip out to Spring Farm in the fall of 1999. My friend Robie and I often take long road trips together to attend holistic classes. One year, we drove to and from California, came home for a week and then drove back to New York (Spring Farm again). We enjoy planning our routes to include stops at zoological gardens, that is, the kind of zoo where the physical and emotional welfare of the residents is given careful consideration. Since Cleveland was conveniently in our path on this jaunt, we'd allowed time for a nice long zoo tour, plus meeting my email pen-pal, Susan, who was working there at the time.

One of the features of Metroparks Zoo is a rain forest exhibit. Inside the building, you climb stairs to the second level (or enter a hollow "tree trunk" and wend your way up the spiral staircase) and walk into an observation post designed to recreate the headquarters of an onsite naturalist. At the far end of this room is a wooden bench underneath a small window looking out on the orangutan enclosure. A gigantic man-made tree dominates the center of the exhibit, giving the orangs space to climb and perch high above the floor.

I leaned over and peered through the two-foot-square window and noticed an adult male, a half-grown youngster, and an adult female orang. I looked at the female and mentally said hello to her. To my amazement, she turned and locked eyes with me from 20 feet away and immediately moved towards me. She climbed into the window frame and gazed into my eyes for at least a minute, then turned and looked Susan in the eye in the same way. Since Susan and I were cramped for space trying to look through the window together, we left the observation hut and walked all around the other rain forest exhibits until we reached the glass-walled front of the orangutan's space.

A plaque on the wall told us our new friend's name was Kayla. As we moved from one pane to the next, Kayla followed us. I'd seen TV footage showing humans and apes interacting through glass or bars, but now I was honored to experience it myself. We'd put a hand flat against the glass and Kayla would put her hand up to ours. I didn't care what any of the other zoo visitors thought, I put my lips to the glass. Kayla "kissed" me from her side of the barrier. The impression that she wanted me to do something kept growing and it occurred to me that she was asking for Reiki healing. I left Susan still communing with Kayla and went to find Robie since she was the only one of us who had then been attuned to give Reiki.

Looking for a little privacy, the three of us went back inside the wooden hut with its little window. Kayla followed and boosted herself onto the sill. We crammed together until we could put our hands to the glass, all at the same time, setting the intention to send her healing, loving energy. Kayla turned away and flattened her back against the window. Once she turned and presented her belly for Reiki, then pressed her back tight to the glass again. Eventually, Susan and I stepped back and left the work to Robie. After a couple more minutes, Robie's back was strained from leaning across the bench in front of the window, so she let her hands fall and she straightened up. Instantly, Kayla's head whipped around to look over her shoulder and her right hand shot up; BAM, BAM, her knuckles hit the glass. You didn't need to be a communicator to comprehend *that* demand and we all jumped to get our hands back up there.

If you've had the pleasure of experiencing any kind of energy- or bodywork, you probably know that you sometimes undergo a "detoxing" as your bodily functions speed up to remove the uprooted wastes from your system. Well, after we resumed sending her energy, Kayla then proceeded to produce a massive pile of detox all over the windowsill. Obviously, our work was done. Since there was no clean space left for her there, we again walked all the way around to the glass wall, and the grateful Kayla met us. This time Robie, too, got to enjoy the handholding and kissies. The attention we were getting from Kayla began to draw a bit of a crowd. I admit to feeling a little smug that she ignored the overtures of all the other onlookers, who were now trying to get a piece of the action, and instead focused only on the three of us—a rewarding confirmation of our special connection with her.

The following year, Robie and I again stopped in Cleveland on the way to more classes at Spring Farm. Of course, our first objective was the zoo and, specifically, the rain forest. I couldn't spot Kayla through the wood-frame window, so I zipped around to the front, anxiously scanning for her. My disappointment turned to elation when I looked up into the tree branches. There she was, looking into my eyes, and reaching her hand out to me as she began to clamber down. I was laughing and crying at the same time as we resumed our friendship despite the glass barrier.

I find it difficult to describe what I saw in Kayla's eyes. There was a calm, a deep peace, in their depths. I was seeing into an old soul. I felt such a bond with her that I truly longed to hug her. To my sorrow, though I've visited the zoo at least twice since then, I haven't seen her again.

There were different orangs on display, though from the zoo's website, I think Kayla is still living there and has in fact had two babies since I last saw her. I hold the hope that I'll have a chance to meet her gaze and be in communion with her again some day.

Heart Talk

"My brother, Connery, and I commune with the Sunlight and weave its living energy into healing. For our family, ourselves, everybody!"

~ *Misha, Karen's cat companion*

12 ~ The Continuity of Love

As an animal communicator, I'm asked to help with practical problems such as explaining to a dog about the responsibility of keeping the house clean and dry (my usual reminder for them is "Poop and pee go out by the tree!") or negotiating with a cat who's less than scrupulous about using the litter box. But the consultations I find most rewarding often occur when my human client is facing the impending transition of a precious animal friend. To be of service as a calm center during this emotionally devastating time is my honor. And then helping reconnect the person with the animal now in spirit is a pure joy.

Over the years, my own animal family has given me plenty of experience with the sorrows of parting with a beloved friend. I'm infinitely grateful never to have lost one to an accident, but we've agonized over healthcare decisions in long-term illness and lost our dear ones in unforeseen, abruptly fatal disease as well. It's not easy in any case. A fleeting life or years spent together, it doesn't matter. The grief is the same. Our animal companions provide us with the closest thing to unconditional love that we can know in this lifetime, and being parted by death can feel like the end of our world. But my animals have also taught me that love lives on in our next companion. Many little ones, dogs in particular, have told me it would break their hearts if their person refused to take in a new animal because their special baby could never be replaced and the pain of loss would be just too much to bear again in the future. They want us to understand the continuity of love. One animal can never replace another, but the quality of the love remains the same. This teaching is one of their gifts to us humans.

I cringe a bit every time someone tells me that the current companion is the "once-in-a-lifetime" dog, cat, or whatever. I felt that way about my first cat, Nortie, but now here's Connery in my life. And each animal has taught me a new aspect of living to the fullest. I treasure them all, past, present, and I'm sure, future.

It's in the most difficult situations that we have the greatest opportunity to learn and grow. Our two "White Dogs of the North" (as David fondly calls them), Angel and Katie, taught me huge lessons. Angel is on the Other Side and at this moment, Katie is curled into a ball with her tail over her nose, five feet from my chair. The challenge they offered me happened three years ago when first Katie, then Angel, became seriously ill.

Katie had shown signs of weakness for several days. A quick visit to the local vet didn't reveal anything, but we were told to watch her. When she began leaking urine, I freaked out and phoned our holistic vet 38 miles away in Des Moines. He tried to reassure me that it was probably a bladder infection, but could be something as serious as kidney problems, so I should bring her right in. A blood test sent me into a panic: Katie's kidneys weren't effectively filtering her blood and toxins were building up in her body. Dr. VanEngelenburg tried to calm me down by telling me that Chinese herbs can often reverse this situation. He gave Katie a laser-acupuncture treatment and sent us home with a supply of Quiet Contemplative pills. But even as Katie failed to improve, Angel became listless. I knew something was horribly wrong when family friends came for a pre-Christmas visit and she failed to get up off the floor to greet them. Another frantic trip to see Dr. Van and another frightening diagnosis—her liver was failing. Lots more pills for both dogs. One of our kitchen cupboards began to resemble a pharmacy.

The thought of losing both our beloved blue-eyed white huskies at the same time was unbearable. It just wasn't fair: though Angel was 12 and had already had a benign lung tumor surgically removed the year before, Kate was only 7 years old! I began taking sick days as my terror manifested as digestive problems. It felt as though the three of us were spiraling down together. I remember passing Connery in our hallway and in my anguish, I cried out, "Connery, why do things have to fall apart?" I really didn't expect an answer, but I heard his calm reply in my mind: "Things fall apart so they can come back together in a new arrangement."

Katie's prognosis was so grim, I decided to explain the process of euthanasia to her so she'd understand that option. I described and visualized the procedure to her. She asked, "What does it feel like?" I told her I didn't know, but she could ask Elke in spirit since that's how she'd left her body. Paranoid that I hadn't gotten my message across, I repeated the visualization, but was interrupted by Katie. She sounded just a little testy: "I *got* it, Mom."

About the time I was sure I was losing my mind, my acupuncturist friend, Valerie, stopped by to assess the herbs we were giving Katie. She looked at both dogs, spoke with me for a few minutes, then gently explained that she felt she was there not to make herbal recommendations, but to point out that my fear and depression were weighing on the girls. Instead of putting their physical and emotional energy into self-healing, they were trying to help *me*. Immediately, I felt the truth of Valerie's words. Thankfully, my intuition kicked in loudly enough for me to get the message to pick up a book I'd purchased months before, but hadn't touched since. That book was *Ask and It Is Given*, by Esther and Jerry Hicks, and the concept that leapt off the page for me is that obsessing on a problem only feeds it more power. I started to make a conscious effort to search for any signs of improvement instead of watching, hawk-like, for further declines in their health. Both dogs perked up as soon as I started to shift my attitude from fearing the worst to hoping for the best.

On the day Katie had a blood test that showed her kidneys were approaching end-stage failure, Dr. Van suggested we try a new probiotic (now marketed as Azodyl) that had just become available. In two weeks, Katie went from requiring a half-bag of subcutaneous fluids every other day to a third of a bag every three days. We could chart her improvement by how hard it became to catch her and hold her still to administer the saline. A follow-up blood test showed her kidney function had improved so much we no longer had to force the hated fluids on her. God bless him, it was David who took it upon himself to do the needle-stick on his little princess for every treatment. This is a sensitive man who can't bear to watch when he (or anyone else) gets a shot or has blood drawn, but he loves the girl so much that he overcame his squeamishness to help save her life.

Angel's energy rebounded miraculously following my attitude adjustment. Though she had a couple of scary relapses, she was able to stay with us for well over a year after the liver diagnosis. I never put her through diagnostic tests to try to pinpoint the cause of the liver deterioration. She'd been through hell when her lungs collapsed due to a tumor leaking air into her chest cavity, followed by the procedure to pump out the air, and then the lung surgery. She made it clear to me that she'd had enough medical intervention. The toughest thing for us to take was the grand mal seizure she'd suffer at least once a month due to slight brain damage probably brought on by the lack of oxygen before the lung problem was diagnosed and corrected. It was wrenching to see her as her sunny self one moment, then turn around and find her down and wildly kicking, gasping, and foaming at the mouth. The aftermath of the seizure was nearly as hard to take. As she'd gradually revive, she'd be completely disoriented and that's when the barking would begin. Following the first few seizures, she'd let out a hoarse bark every five seconds for a solid two hours. As we used holistic treatments on her, the barking time reduced to under an hour, but she'd still be restless and agitated for another 24 hours.

I remember going to see *Eight Below* (the story of sled dogs abandoned in the Antarctic) in a theater during Angel's last year. Honestly, it wasn't very entertaining for me as I sat and sobbed all the way through the movie. It brought up all the helplessness I felt whenever Angel was seizing and I could only stand by and pray that she'd live through it one more time. I began using energy healing techniques on her after it became obvious we were going to have to deal with seizures the rest of her life, but I'm not sure how much they helped. We couldn't give her the Phenobarbital commonly prescribed to control seizures because her liver function was already compromised. At least the energy work made me feel as though I were doing *something* for her.

In late April of 2006, Angel's appetite disappeared. Nothing could tempt her to eat. The weakness and lethargy returned and this time we could sense she wasn't going to bounce back. I had a brief day of renewed hope when she ate some stale tortillas I'd tossed outside for the birds.

She then gladly accepted some soft dog treats and my spirits soared, but by evening the emotional roller coaster plummeted back down as she suffered violent vomiting. That day was the last time she even tried to eat.

Before I learned animal communication, my philosophy about euthanasia was "the sooner, the better." I never thought about it hard enough to wonder whether it was for the good of the animal, or so *I* wouldn't have to deal with my companion's process of transition. As Sharon Callahan mentored me, she taught me that "the greatest gift we can give our animals is to mid-wife the dying process." Angel was very clear about her wishes: She wanted to experience her natural transition without euthanasia. And she wanted me to be present with her. Her challenge to me was, "Treasure every moment we have together without trying to guess how many are left." She instructed me to pull a tuft of her fur from the left side of her thick white ruff and put it in my medicine bag. She told me to take another tuft from the right side for my bag once she'd left her body. "You'll notice there's no difference," she said.

I was terrified that Angel would leave in the midst of a horrific seizure and I couldn't bear the thought. Though I did notice a couple of neurological glitches that caused her to lose her footing, she never had another grand mal episode. Her preference was to remain outside most of the time as it became harder and harder for her to navigate bare floors in the house. My torment continued to revolve around the euthanasia question. Was I hearing her correctly? David pointed out the window one evening as a pale peach sunset tinted the sky. There sat Angel, facing west and gazing up into the glow. David and I shed a few tears together and I knew I *was* following her wishes.

As we neared the end of the week, I again asked Angel to let me know whether she wanted euthanasia. This time, she agreed that I could take her to the vet when the time was right. I tried to negotiate with her... could I make an appointment for Saturday morning since the vet would be out the rest of the weekend? I heard her reply in the familiar, matter-of-fact tone, "You can't put a deadline on my transition." I laughed in spite of myself. Here I'm petrified and she's making jokes!

Angel stayed with us through that weekend and most of the day on Monday. Late in the afternoon, I heard her give a strange, hoarse cry from the backyard and I ran outside to find her lying there. Obviously, she could no longer get to her feet. Thank God, our next-door neighbor got home just as I was fretting over how to move Angel out of the hot sun, into the house. We pulled her onto a blanket and carried her inside. She told me it was now OK to take her to the vet.

As soon as David got home from work, I met him at the front door and told him Angel was on her way out. Weak though she was, she still lifted her head to greet him with a smile when he walked into the kitchen where she lay. Together we carried her on the blanket to the car. My best friend, Robie, met us at the vet clinic so she could say goodbye to Angel, who was just able to acknowledge her presence. Dr. Rizzo and her staff had stayed late for us and everything was already prepared. Moments later, Angel was released from her body. As I knelt by her, I followed her instructions and took a pinch of fur from the right side of her ruff. It's in my medicine bag along with the fur from the left side, and of course she was right...I can't tell one tuft from the other.

As I mourned Angel in the following days, I honored her for all the experiential lessons she gave me during her almost-14-year life. And an old question began to nag at me, one that hadn't seemed all that relevant until now. I took my conundrum to my favorite sage, Mr. C. "Connery," I said, "please explain something to me. I completely trust that all my animals will be waiting for me when I cross over. Yet I also fully believe that reincarnation is real. How do you reconcile the two?"

His reply was one of the most beautiful things I've ever heard from an animal. He told me, "What waits for you on the Other Side is an energetic imprint of the animal you knew and loved. It's as though all the love you shared leaves an imprint. You don't have a word for it since it's an energy thing and you don't understand that very well. 'Hologram' is the closest term. But that's inaccurate because it implies that it isn't real and this *is* real." He went on to say, "The animal's soul is then free to travel on and can reincarnate and even come back to you in a new form."

I was blown away by Connery's information. I didn't quite trust that I'd understood him correctly on something this important, so I contacted Dawn Hayman at Spring Farm. I'll always think of Dawn as my primary animal communication teacher since it was under her tutelage that I had my first successes. I was elated when Dawn agreed that many animals have told her the same thing over the years. What a comforting concept Angel's passing had brought into my awareness. I felt even more gratitude for Angel and Connery.

Some months after this revelation, I was talking by phone with Linda, a client whose beloved cat, Sunny, had crossed over a couple of years before. Linda likes to check in with her cat's spirit from time to time, waiting for the day she can be done with her travel obligations and settle at home to hope for a reincarnated reunion with her friend. As I struggled to interpret Connery's explanation for Linda, her cat jumped in to clarify. "Look at it this way: I'll be waiting for you, yet Sunny 2.1 can come and live with you." Linda and I laughed together—A perfect analogy to describe the new, reincarnated version of an animal companion.

Lotus and Sunny

Prior to Misha and Connery, David and I also had a cat named Sunny, short for Silver Sun. He and his little "sister," Lotus, were Korats, an exotic-looking breed of silvery gray kitties with huge eyes and ears. Sunny was David's special pal. We often reminisce about his antics and get a little misty-eyed. We can't help smiling when we speak of the time we fixed a wonderful barbecue and shared a little with the cats (who were our only kids at the time). Sunny was so pleased with the food, our company, and the mellow mood of the afternoon, he crawled up into David's arms and began grooming himself. After a thorough paw-licking and whisker-washing, he lazily stretched up and meticulously groomed the big, thick mustache that David wore in those days. Sunny then fell into a peaceful snooze on David's chest.

I'm compelled to share Sunny's most endearing trait, at least in *my* opinion. Even though he was "David's cat," he would never tolerate David tickling me. If we were sitting on the couch and David suddenly grabbed a ticklish spot on me, Sunny would appear out of nowhere and squeeze in between us, an anxious look on his face. One day, I said something snotty to David and he chased me through our apartment, digging his fingers into my ribcage. In between my shrieks of involuntary laughter, I warned him that my attack cat would get him. He snorted at that and kept right on tormenting me. Next moment, he was the one doing the yelling as Sunny ran up behind him and bit him on the ankle.

Lotus was a sweet, diminutive girl and Sunny enjoyed play-pummeling her on a regular basis. But at least once a week, Lotus would have her fill of that and proceed to kick Sunny's rather fat ass. Every time he'd try to get to his feet and escape, she'd tackle him and knock him flat again.

It was Sunny and Lotus who taught David all about the concept of the continuity of love.

After his nearly life-long companion, Lotus, succumbed to kidney failure, Sunny started going downhill, too. I dreaded the time he would leave us because I knew how difficult his passing would be, especially for David. As it became obvious we'd soon have to make a decision about Sunny, I mentioned to David that I was actually looking forward to some time without having to care for cats. The Korats had always been somewhat high-maintenance, with chronic health problems that flared up once a year or more. Poor Lotus spent her entire life as a bulimic, eating heartily for a couple of days and throwing up every bite the next. I wish I'd known more about animal nutrition in those days. But as soon as Sunny left his body, I began to miss feline energy in our house. I dearly loved our huskies, but things seemed out of balance. I forged ahead with my plan to find my gray tiger kittens, strong little moggies who would be healthier than the purebred Korats (so much for that idea in the case of Jackie!). David was less enthusiastic about adopting new cats.

Sunny passed in late spring; Connery and his brothers joined the household in early September. Although David enjoyed the kittens and certainly did his part to take care of them, he seemed reluctant to form a deep bond with them. He mourned Jackie's passing, of course, but it didn't have the same overwhelming impact on him that it had on me. By December, I was getting frustrated that David still felt it would be disloyal to Sunny's memory to develop a connection with Misha and Connery.

I'd recently contracted with Susan Marino (who later became the co-founder of Angel's Gate Hospice for Animals) to communicate with our cats and dogs. It was my first experience with animal communication and I found it fascinating and exciting. I then got the bright idea of asking Sue for another appointment to ask our animals for messages for David. I'd write them up and give them to him in a notebook as a Christmas present.

When I asked for Sunny's words for David, I expected Sue to give me all sorts of lovey-dovey sentiments. Instead, she told me, "Sunny is frustrated with David." As I reeled in surprise, she elaborated. "He's frustrated that David doesn't believe he's still there." She paused for a moment, then added, "OK. I've asked Sunny to give David a sign. Then David will be better able to accept the new cats."

Christmas arrived less than a week later. David and I were celebrating with his parents in their home. As the gift exchange wound down, I handed David the notebook I'd prepared for him. I'm not sure what I was expecting, but I was amazed when he read it and burst into tears, which he quickly concealed from his parents. He whispered to me that he'd explain later. On the drive home, he told me about the experience he'd had the very night after Sue suggested that Sunny give him a sign of his presence. He was lying in bed and one of the kittens climbed under the covers with him, but didn't stay long. Though Lotus and Sunny adored sleeping under the blankets with us (Lotus invariably with all four little ice-cube paws pressed up against a human thigh), Misha and Connery prefer to sleep on top of us. David began to feel a warm weight next to his feet. He was puzzled because he was sure the kitten had left.

Wondering what was happening, David reached down to touch the apparent cat under the covers by his feet, but there was nothing there. The warmth quickly dissipated. He hadn't really thought any more about this odd experience until he read the animal communication notebook. Suddenly, he understood that this had been the sign Sue had asked Sunny to give him. Thus his sudden tears.

There's a bit more to this story. That Christmas night, the kittens crawled into bed with David, and stayed only a minute. Again, David knew there were no cats under the covers. In fact, he could hear both of them chasing and feisting (as we call kitty wrestling matches) across the bedroom from him. But he could *feel* feline weight and warmth next to his feet. This time, he held very still and marveled at the presence of his precious, "departed" cat companions. In his mind, he said, "Thank you, Sunny and Lotus!" He told me the next morning that the warmth became so intense that he had to pull the blanket off his shoulder so he could cool off a little. Gradually, the sensation faded away and David fell asleep, feeling more comforted than he had in the months since Sunny's transition.

As that continuity of love prevailed, David opened his heart to the new cats and became Misha's mentor, teaching him how to enjoy living in a cat body by playing with him and helping him learn to enjoy human attention. These days, Misha especially adores his Dad and demands his morning cuddle-session with loud yowls, standing up on his hind legs on the kitchen counter, reaching out for David as he tries to get ready for work. And Lotus and Sunny live on in our hearts.

Heart Talk

I asked for dream guidance before sleeping one night. I came back with the concept: "The purpose of Light is to illuminate Love." The word "illuminate" carried the sense of permeating every dark corner, not with blinding light, but soft, iridescent white light. The Light of God's Love.

~ Karen

13 ~ An Orange Cat Miracle

Herschel, a magnificent example of an orange cat, was born to a feral mother inside the apartment wall of my client, Kim. Kim tells me she was even present at his conception on the day she was late for work because Buddy, the orange Manx "everybody's cat" of the apartment house, was copulating with the stray female on the hood of Kim's car. When the kittens were born, she could hear them mewing inside the wall, but couldn't get to them. After Mom decided to move the four kittens during a flooding rain, Kim rescued them from a landscaping berm surrounded by water. The local shelter told Kim they would euthanise them because they were too young and weak. Horrified, Kim took back the two stronger kittens and Herschel (who was named not for football star Herschel Walker, but after a venerable architect in the firm where Kim was interning) and his brother Elmo then became *her* babies.

She bottle-fed them and provided badly needed vet care and when they were old enough, advertised to find them homes since she was intending to move to another city. The people who came to see them paid no attention to Herschel, who always seemed to keep a low profile while they were there, but Elmo was soon adopted. When Kim discovered that her little orange pal loved to ride with her in the car, she quit trying to find another home for him and faced the fact that they were meant for each other.

Her efforts and loving attention were rewarded with his companionship and good humor for the duration of his long life. "And beyond," he chimes in from Spirit. Herschel rode in the car with Kim when she relocated from Dallas to Seattle, and he was the tender age of six weeks at the time. He adored fetching toys she'd throw for him and she'd often wake in the morning to find a half dozen of them lying next to her. Kim described to me their many adventures, laughing as she recalled the time they lived in Canada where Herschel grew a "ridiculously dense" coat. (As I type this, Herschel sends me a mental picture of himself as a cold, disgruntled cat huddled inside a fur parka. "Not enough sun warmth there," he says.) He would amuse Kim by patting her lips with his paws, "as though he were trying to climb into my mouth."

Kim came to rely on Herschel to screen potential boyfriends for her. She'd quickly realized that any guy her cat didn't like wasn't worth dating. When she brought home new friend, Will, for Herschel to check out, it was mutual delight. The cat was "all over him" and Will loved it, which Kim took as a very good sign. Such was Herschel's status as an honored family member that as the relationship blossomed, Will asked for his approval to marry Kim.

Herschel gleefully included Will in the orange cat games. One night, the three of them were taking turns jumping out and "scaring" each other. After a few minutes, Herschel apparently lost interest in the game, so his humans went off to bed. As they were falling asleep, out of nowhere, Herschel leapt right on top of Kim. She recalls, "As he smiled and capered off, Will and I hooted with laughter as he *really* did scare me!"

I was introduced to Herschel in his waning months. Kim wanted to know how much medical intervention he'd accept or whether he preferred to be left to his own natural transition process. It was a rough emotional time for Kim, but she followed all of Herschel's wishes and saw him safely to the Other Side. She was with him "cradle to grave," as Herschel put it. I can understand how he was just like another person in the family from the remarks he's made to me, especially since his passing. For example, when I mentioned to Kim that our animals are able to access any book or article that their humans have read, she said, "Then Herschel must have been a very well-read cat since I was a literature major." As I hung up the phone, he popped into my mind and commented, "I'm partial to Thomas Hardy." I emailed this transmission to Kim and got an excited reply that she and Will used to joke about which authors Herschel would most appreciate and Hardy had been one of the two finalists.

By the time of Herschel's passing, the family had grown by two human children, two more cats, parakeets, and a dog. But his departure left a gaping hole and Kim felt drawn to look for orange kittens. She inundated me with photographs of potential adoptees and also asked for Herschel's input on which would be the most suitable addition. With his help, we narrowed it down to a specific litter comprised of five orangies housed in foster care in Houston, four hours' drive from Kim and Will's home in Dallas. When Kim went to see the kittens, she debated about taking more than one, but ended up choosing a male named Ziggy. He was quickly re-christened Zachariah and instantly became a beloved part of the family.

The only "problem" with Zach was his extreme zest for life. The older cats were overwhelmed with his energy and constant quest for a playmate. The foster family was so thrilled that Kim wanted to adopt one (or more, they hoped) of Zach's siblings, they drove the whole bunch to Dallas. I got a frantic call from Kim, telling me that orange kittens were bouncing off the walls and Zach was furious. Indignantly, he told me, "I got my home. They can go find their own!" I checked in with Herschel who suggested that Kim should choose between sisters, "Sweet Pepper" and "Freedom" and send the rest of the lot home. From his perspective on the Other Side, Herschel assured her that either kitten would blend well with the existing family, but he told Kim that if she wanted a challenge, she'd select Freedom. So rebel that she is, Kim chose to adopt Freedom.

In her first few days in the household, Freedom told Will she wanted to be named Lydia. And Lydia proved Herschel's assessment correct. Her ravenous appetite nearly drove Kim nuts as she'd launched herself into the air, knocking the food bowls out of Kim's hands. Turns out it was no wonder she was constantly starved: She needed all that food to grow to her full size. She soon became a long, tall, armload of an orange cat, no fat and all muscle.

I recall I did quite a few consultations for Kim as she tried to sort out life with Lydia in the family. Kim complained that when she'd try to read a story book to her daughter with the little girl seated on her lap, Lydia would try to squirm in there, too (difficult since she's bigger than a lapdog). I told Kim that Lydia wanted to hear the story and see the pictures, too, and suggested they all sit on a couch together so there'd be room for the three of them. Bless Kim's heart, she didn't laugh at this advice, but tried it out and story time became peaceful again. She told me she'd show the picture to her daughter, then angle the book for Lydia to see. We marveled at Lydia's fascination with children's books. If a pop-up book were left on the floor, Lydia would open it and watch the illustrations spring up, then she'd close and reopen it, over and over.

Zach and Lydia became inseparable playmates, wearing each other out with insane chases throughout the house. While Lydia was the wild-woman, Zach earned the nickname Pooh because of his snuggly, loving nature. He endeared himself to Kim and Will by waving his paws at their baby son whenever they carried Zach into the nursery to visit him.

I didn't hear from Kim for several months and heaved a sigh of relief that things must be stabilizing at last (though I missed the fabulous tales from their multi-species household). But the next email I got from her brought horrible news: Zach was seriously ill. They sought allopathic and holistic treatment for him. The allopathic vet had no clue what had caused Zach's weakness and multiple seizures, but the holistic vet suspected over-vaccination. When animals are brought into the shelter/ foster systems, the practice is to err on the side of caution and vaccinate when there are no records to go on. Some animals' systems are far too sensitive to be subjected to multiple vaccinations and apparently this was the case with Zach.

Kim and Will fought hard for Zach, taking turns getting up every hour during the night to administer homeopathics to him. The other cats kept vigil with him except when he was seizing, which proved to be too much for them to tolerate. He'd rally for a while, then his energy would wane again. Ultimately, he left his body just before dawn one morning.

When I asked for guidance concerning Zach's brief lifetime, I received the message that much like my own little Jackie kitten, his mission was to study and experience the depths of human compassion. He had come to be with them to learn and then return to spirit to "report in." He told me he could have tried to stay in his body, but that it was so badly damaged that he would have had frequent seizures as long as he lived and that would have been too hard on his human and feline family. I strongly felt Zach and Herschel together on the Other Side. Every time I tuned in to them, I got a sense of conspiracy and lots of giggling. Some great plot was being hatched, I felt sure, but they weren't letting me in on it.

Kim told me Lydia was going crazy without her playmate, and dragging everyone else with her. Zach told me he'd try to keep Lydia occupied in his spirit form until they could find a new kitten to distract her. The day after I got that message from Zach, Kim emailed and said that Will had called her into the room to watch Lydia. She was leaping and rolling as though playing with another cat. Then she'd tear from room to room; obviously Spirit Zach was chasing her.

Still Lydia's boundless energy made it imperative to bring in a new young cat to engage her. Soon the adoptable orange kitten photos began arriving in my inbox again. In the batch was a cute little guy of whom Kim said, "I squeaked when I saw his picture." I took that as a hint to look closely at this one. His name was Forrest, Kim told me, and he'd been in foster care for weeks. Her fear was that he wouldn't be enough cat to take on Lydia because although he was six months old, he was more the size of a kitten two months younger than that. He was as petite as Lydia was strapping. I once again promised to consult Herschel and now Zach, as well.

I tuned into the two of them and asked for their assessment of Forrest as a potential family member and a foil for Lydia in particular. Zach assured me that Forrest would be able to take on Lydia. Then they explained the situation to me. Forrest, they said, was being animated by a "seed spirit" who would let Zach take over the body. Zach would become what's known in metaphysical circles as a "walk-in." The seed spirit would return to the Other Side and let Zach reincarnate in the new, ready-made body. Kim would need only to make a connection with Forrest and commit to taking him home for everything to fall into perfect order.

I could sense Herschel and Zach laughing at my astonishment and my linear thinking. "All this has been in place for ages," they told me. They elaborated that a seed spirit is like a placeholder to allow for the immediate return of a beloved animal's soul to its former family. Forrest, they told me, was healthy, but not yet very strong because the seed spirit isn't fully grounded in the body in order to expedite the spirits' exchange. But they stressed that when Zach (that is, Zach 2.1) takes over, the Forrest-form will begin to strengthen. I asked whether this is a common occurrence among animals and they told me it *is* fairly common, but especially among orange cats. My impression is that if the body of a seed spirit goes unclaimed, the spirit simply returns to the Other Side and the body dies.

Even though they'd shared these revelations with me, I again had the impression that H and Z were snickering conspiratorially behind my back. I let that feeling go and went about conveying their message to Kim. Bottom line, all she'd have to do was look for a spark between herself and Forrest and then she'd *know* he was the right cat.

Kim called me the next day and said she'd spoken with Forrest's foster mom. The woman had actually tried to dissuade Kim from coming to see him, "because he has such a nothing-personality." In fact, to Kim's dismay, he'd been named after Forrest Gump. But when Kim arrived three days later to meet him, the foster mom mentioned that it was odd, but the kitten had "started to come around" shortly after Kim made the appointment. God, I love how these pageants unfold! I came home that day to a voice mail from Kim that delighted me to the point that I left it on the machine for weeks, listening to it whenever I needed a laugh. She was giggling so hard I could barely make out her words. "I'm driving home with the little Forrest next to me and he's purring. When I met him, he patted me on the chin and I took that as a good sign. But he's tiny! I hope Lydia doesn't eat him for lunch!"

Kim was not happy with her new fur-child's namesake and he was soon given a dignified, Old English name, Perkyn. They made him comfy in their computer room so he could be introduced to the family individually, for his own safety. Arvin the dog, Lydia, Elgin and Lexi, the cats, could watch him through the French doors. He and the children instantly hit it off, and things seemed to go well with the other critters…except Lydia. I got another desperate email, but this time with an unexpected crisis. While Kim anxiously watched, Lydia had stretched her long arm under the door, groping around for Perkyn. To Kim's horror, Perkyn puffed up, charged straight for Lydia and pounced on her arm with all four paws. I roared with laughter when I tuned into Perkyn: "No one's going to eat *me* for lunch!"

We quickly got that sorted out as I explained Mom had only been joking about Lydia eating him. And now Perkyn had established that he was no pushover. The way was clear for Lydia and Perkyn to bond, and bond they did. Furry orange lightning bolts were once again zinging through the house in the mad game of cat-tag, just as in the days of Zach and Lydia. But there was one more call from Kim, this time to share the miracle with me.

As they got to know Perkyn better, Will and Kim began noticing very familiar peculiarities. Carrying the kitten in to say goodnight to the baby, Perkyn would wave his paws at him. And he'd pat at Kim's mouth as though he were trying to climb into it. The more they compared notes, the more they realized that Perkyn exhibited trademark behaviors not only of Zach, but of Herschel, as well. Perkyn's eyes are gold around the pupil and green around the iris edge, yet when he'd show a Zach trait, his eyes took on an all-gold appearance similar to Zach's coppery golden eyes. And his eyes flashed all green, reflecting the eyes of Herschel, whenever a beloved Herschel trick materialized.

In awe, I turned to Zach and Herschel in spirit and was given a beautiful mental image of a golden light ray emanating from Zach and a ray of brilliant blue from Herschel, uniting into glowing emerald and beaming straight into Perkyn. The full conspiracy finally revealed: Perkyn carries a spark of both Zach *and* Herschel. While he's his own man, the love of their previous cats lives on for Kim and Will, embodied by the plucky little Perkyn.

Heart Talk

"Life is a circle, but you don't have to spin."

~ Annie Perry, gray goose at Spring Farm CARES

14 - Come...Come to Spring Farm

As a kid, I recall being irritated when adults would make conversation with me by asking, "And what do *you* want to be when you grow up?" They always seemed so amused if I told them I guessed I'd be a writer or an artist. It gave me the feeling they were chuckling behind my back and saying to the other adults, "Oh, isn't that just precious?" Honestly, I didn't really know *what* I wanted to be; certainly nothing sensible rang my chimes. Then, when I was about ten years old, I watched *The Three Lives of Thomasina* on the Walt Disney TV show. There I saw my role model. I wanted to grow up to be Lori MacGregor, the supposed "witch" who could charm and heal animals.

I was old enough to know better than tell anybody I wanted to grow up to be a fictional character, but tales of communing with animals filled my daydreams (at least in addition to pining for romance). For a while, I entertained thoughts of weaving beautiful cloth on a gigantic wood-frame loom (just like Lori in the movie), but gave up that fantasy when I learned of the tedious job of threading the thing.

So for 20 years, I'd plodded along in a secure, sensible state job, complete with great benefits, when I got a call from my older sister, Mary. She told me of meeting a real, live animal communicator at a spiritual development class they'd both been taking. Mary was excited. She said the woman taught classes on how to learn to talk with animals, and she lived only 20 minutes away from Mary's home on Long Island. I could come out for a visit and take the workshop, too.

As I've mentioned, I was pessimistic about the idea that I could do animal communication, but Mary persisted. She reminded me that I'd been able to hear Nortie, the amazing golden-eyed black cat with the bobbed-off tail whom I'd inherited from Mary when she and her husband moved overseas for several years. True, I had heard a couple of brief things from Nortie, but I gave her all the credit for that. She was an incredible soul who just happened to inhabit a cat body.

I decided that at least I'd phone this woman, Susan Marino, and set up a consultation for our dogs and cats. Sue was wonderful, though I tested her unmercifully, and she warmed my enthusiasm enough for me to consider making the long drive from Iowa to New York. So eventually, my friend, Robie, and I came to make our first animal communication workshop road trip.

Honestly, I don't think I really was able to "get" anything from any of Susan's many animal friends, but I basked in the atmosphere of her home and marveled at the ease with which she obviously connected with all their dogs and cats, and the varied (and extremely noisy) collection of macaws, parrots, and the single, somewhat ornery, cockatoo (who went after my fingers instead of the fruit I was offering him). I recognized Susan as a true Earth Angel, so filled with compassion that she lived completely in service to the animals. I wasn't surprised to hear later that she and her partner, Vic, had turned their property into the Angel's Gate Hospice for Animals.

Throughout the workshop, Susan insisted that anyone with the desire and the commitment could learn to be an animal communicator. My childhood dream was suddenly revived.

Among Susan's recommendations for those wanting to learn to communicate telepathically with animals was to take classes from as many different teachers as possible. Everyone has a personal approach and you pick up various facets from each one. "If you have a chance to work with Dawn Hayman at Spring Farm, *take it,*" she told our class.

A year or so later, the synchronicities kicked in and purely "by chance" a communicator with whom I'd formed an e-mail pen-pal relationship mentioned that Dawn would be teaching a weekend workshop in Missouri. And that became the class that proved to be my breakthrough. You've already heard the story about my recruitment by orange cat, Sonya Pia. But the very first animal I was able to hear during that workshop was the little black pug who lived at the retreat center where we were meeting.

Our assignment was to seek out one of the resident critters and just say hello, and "imagine hearing 'hello' back." I found "Pugsley" sitting near the basement bathroom, waiting for his human mom to get out of the shower. I parked next to him and began massaging the top of his head, but when I moved down to rub his shoulders, I thought I heard a voice in my mind: "Ooh, the head, the head!" I chalked it up to body language and went back to working around his ears.

At that moment, fierce barking erupted outside the glass door nearby. I saw "Mark Russell," the Jack Russell terrier, flash past the door. (Much to our amusement, we'd been told during class that this dog insisted on being called by his full name, not just "Mark" or "Russell."). That was when I distinctly heard Pugsley say, with infinite disdain, "And that Mark Russell! Running around like an *idiot!*"

Of course, I reported Pugsley's remark when class resumed. Dawn and Pugsley's mom exchanged a knowing look and a chuckle, and Dawn said, "Pugsley has *issues* with Mark Russell."

Wow! I'd gotten it. This works, it's real. The bonfire was ignited. I recall thinking with surprise, "This is easy!" My sweetheart husky, Angel, immediately popped into my mind and I heard her telepathic voice for the very first time: "Of *course* it's easy!" She sounded pretty exasperated, and with no wonder; she'd been working to get me to hear her for ages. And it was later that same morning that Sonya Pia and I made our connection, completely convincing me that animal communication is a reality *and* that I could do it.

I followed Sonya's marching orders and six months later Robie and I were at Spring Farm CARES, attending Dawn's second-level workshop. I'd come to the farm filled to the brim with expectations of miraculous encounters with animals. I had visions of filling notebooks with information and even poetry, dictated to me by the animal master teachers there. After all, I'd heard Sonya so clearly in Missouri, all the way from upstate New York. Surely my success would be even more spectacular here on her home turf.

We arrived hours early for the lecture held the evening before the workshop, just so we could look around. The ubiquitous Spring Farm ducks milled around the yard or snoozed in the late afternoon sunlight. We didn't walk down to the barn, but instead went up the steps onto the open porch of the big gray building. The sign above the double doors read "Kigercat Hall." Near the doors stood a battered easy chair, with an elderly orange cat resting on the seat. Could this really be Sonya Pia? I eased into the chair next to her and she instantly responded by climbing into my lap. I discerned not a single thought from her, but her rumbling purr, delighted murmurs, and many kisses told me I'd found my recruiter, in person. I was being profusely thanked for showing up.

That workshop was an education, indeed. A humbling education. I anticipated having casual conversations, left and right, but my ego was getting in the way of my heart. On our first assignment to go out on the grounds and speak with an animal, I made a beeline to the stall of "Poppy Jay." She was a retired racehorse and she was so badly foundered that she rarely got to her feet. Her condition was gradually improving with holistic care, but her hooves were still far too painful for her to stand on them for more than a few minutes, several times a day. But even lying there on her side, she looked like a queen.

I stood at the fence of her enclosure in the barn arena and *tried* to hear her answers to my questions. Discouraged after several minutes with no contact, I mentally said to her, "Poppy, I'm just not hearing you. Maybe I better try talking with someone else." Her reaction terrified me. She threw her head back over her shoulder to look at me, whinnying and pawing at the sawdust as though attempting to get up. She obviously didn't want me to leave. To appease Poppy Jay, I stayed where I was and she calmed down again. I felt so much compassion for her, my heart was now truly open and *then* I began to hear her telepathic voice. And what she told me had such a profound effect on me that I posted her words on my cubicle wall at work after I got back home. She said, "Release your expectations. They get in the way."

Despite Poppy's excellent advice, I went through much of the workshop beating myself up for not hearing animal after animal. Toward the end of the class, I walked out to the barn, hoping to commune with either of the two llamas, Gulliver and Coriander, or maybe Simon, the white goat. I sat down in a pile of hay and hopefully reached out with my mind to everyone there. Within two minutes, the sheep, the goats, and Gulliver had all cleared out to the pasture, leaving me alone with Coriander. I closed my eyes and attempted to open my heart, but no voice came to my mind. Every once in awhile, I'd open my eyes and look at Corrie. Each time, he was watching me, calmly chewing away at his feed. I felt so disappointed, I was sure he was transmitting messages to me that I wasn't able to hear.

Dejected, I got up and wandered out into the arena. Sitting on a huge pile of clean sawdust, I did hear a few snippets of telepathic talk. A chicken radiating a sense of motherly compassion pecked the floor near me. I heard her tell me, "Be one of the family." But mostly, I listened with my physical ears. Light rain was pattering on the metal roof. The horses stabled to my right whinnied to those on my left, who whinnied back. The chickens murmured to themselves and made little scuffling noises as they scratched in the sawdust. Goats and ponies moved quietly in their stalls as they ate.

Gradually, I began to *feel* the loving community here in this barn, and outward through the entire property. The heart connection between all the animals and all the humans living and working there became clear to me. I experienced a sense of belonging, of being a part of All That Is.

I returned home after that workshop feeling humble and grateful to be accepted into that community. But my ego kept nagging that I should have been able to "get" more from the animal teachers. That's when I read on the Spring Farm website that Penelope Smith would be coming to teach classes there. Here was my chance to complete Sonya Pia's instructions by working with Penelope as well as Dawn. I signed up for her upper-level course and the professional course, back to back.

Early in the first workshop, Penelope led us on a tour to meet all the animals. Back at Kigercat Hall, she instructed us to speak with the very first animal to come to mind. Immediately, I realized Corrie the white llama was the one reaching out to me. With a mental groan, I tried to push him away, telling him I wasn't able to hear him last year so why should this be any different? But the image of him persisted, so I gave up.

All the others left the building to be with the animals, but I stayed behind in the huge empty hall. With a sigh, I began to ask Corrie the practice questions Penelope had provided. And *I heard his answers.* This is my transcript from my journal:

Communication from Coriander the Llama

Sept. 26, 2000

Q. What have you to teach me?
A. Being—you know that!

Q. What do you like about being a llama?
A. The spiritual enlightenment.

Q. What is your greatest joy in life?
A. Teaching; connecting; demonstrating how to BE.
   (Go deeper and meet me. No, not asleep!)

Q. What do you like about your environment?
A. The sacredness.

Q. What is your viewpoint of me?
A. You're searching; search deeper inside yourself. I like your energy.

Q. What do you see as my purpose?
A. You're a teacher, too, but you have to teach yourself first.

Q. What don't you understand about me?
A. How you can be so scattered. So afraid. Gather your power, your energies. Put them to good use. Speaking our truth, telling the world. Healing. You are a healer, you know. Quit denying it. You tell yourself lies about your unworthiness. You have to start being honest with yourself; own your talents. Synergize them into your new life, then step right into it. Stop doubting! The world needs you. The world needs every piece of love. Yes, you are hearing me this time. You heard me last time, too. *I gave you a meditation on oneness.*

I blurted out, "God bless you, Corrie!" The tears were streaming down my face. I heard his calm voice reply, "God blesses us all. Always believe that. You have it, now put it all together."

In a momentary panic, I cried out, "I'm losing the connection!"

Corrie replied, "You just think you are. Stop thinking!" And then he spoke the telepathic words that made him my beloved Dalai Llama: "Stillness is the key. Unlock your heart."

With those simple statements, Corrie summarized the core components of telepathic communication with animals. Being able to cultivate a mind quiet enough to hear the subtle whispers of information is one requirement. Equally important is completely opening your heart to the animal. Being fully present and centered in the moment is also a necessity. Animals live in the "now," and you have to meet them there. I find a sense of peace and timelessness when I'm in that space.

Heart Talk

"We, your cats, both those in form and those in spirit, work together with you. Trying to bring you peace, to quell your fear. Connery says you think too much. Very true. Listen to your llama— you quote him all the time without hearing him in your heart's depth. You're like a mirror reflecting our teachings to everyone else without first taking them into yourself.

Have patience. Don't pounce on [our lessons] like gems/treasures to be doled out. Reflect on them, don't just reflect them. Absorb their meanings systemically. Hold them to your heart, not only to your ears. Feel their truth, don't just hear it. Then you may share them with others."

~ the spirit of Nortie, Karen's late cat companion

15 ~ Listening With Your Heart

Karen:

Many helpful books describing the how-to of animal communication have been published. I've listed a few of my favorites in the resource section at the back of this book. But Connery and I will share some suggestions here to get you started.

Connery:

Now the fun begins! Dust off your imagination skills and enjoy yourself. The "mistake" most people make is being so deadly serious about the whole thing. They want so badly to hear the animals that they block off the energy by trying too hard. As Karen says, you have to (metaphorically) lean back in your chair, open your arms wide and *allow* the communication to happen. It's a matter of fine-tuning in, not forcing yourself to concentrate. It's all about opening up, not clamping down.

When you give your dog a biscuit, do you say, "You're welcome," to the appreciative look you get? Do you say out loud what your cat must be thinking judging from the look on his face? When you're delayed getting home and your animals are grumpy about it, do you find yourself explaining why you were late? If so, in any of these examples, you're doing animal communication. Now, the skeptics would say you're making it up based on your animal's body language, but I submit that the information you start to get as you practice is much more detailed than what could be inferred by posture and expression. The trick is to bring it into your conscious awareness instead of brushing it off.

In the case where you were late coming home and got a reproachful look from your dog: You begin to apologize and explain what happened. Now, if you pause for a moment, close your mouth, and let your mind be still, you'll mentally hear the question, "Where *were* you, anyway?"

Oh, and by the way, if you *are* going to be late, you can take a quiet moment and send your animals a telepathic message to let them know when you'll be home. Otherwise, all they'll pick up on is your agitation and that makes them worry about you.

✋ Karen:

Telepathic messages are usually fleeting and subtle. The transmission is nearly always the very first thing that comes to your mind. If you have to think about it too hard, you've missed it. Go back and recapture that very first thought. You can always politely ask the animal for a clarification if you can't comprehend the message. It can be helpful to ask your question and then write down what ever comes into your mind. Your job is to select the words that best convey the sensations you receive from the animal. Writing it down keeps your brain busy and out of the way while your heart listens.

🐾 Connery:

Ah, I can hear your frustration now: *"But just exactly **how** can I listen with my heart?"* I'd say it's more of a matter of feeling the message with your heart and whole body, and then letting it form a picture in your mind. That could be a visual picture, sounds, emotions, or the "picture" could take the shape of words. Karen uses guided meditation in her classes to help her students open their hearts; that is, allow their hearts' energy to expand. You sense the animals' information via this energy field. And we animal companions help you with this anytime you allow yourself to commune with us; that is, mindfully spend time with us. No shopping lists allowed to pop up at the back of your mind!

Meditation practice is a wonderful way to set your mind aside so the heart's wisdom can speak instead. This does not necessarily mean sitting in the lotus position for hours on end. You can allow yourself to fall into a meditative state while walking or doing simple repetitive chores like dishwashing. The angelic Sharon Callahan chooses not to teach animal communication, but instead helps her students learn to meditate since that quiet, fully present state is the foundation of telepathic communication. Your animals (especially cats and, so I'm told, horses) enjoy being with you during meditation.

✋ Karen:

I personally experience meditation as a state where I can leave my mind-chatter in another room and go somewhere quiet. I can still vaguely hear it yammering away, but if it gets too loud, I merely refocus on my breath or a mantra. Being out in nature is a magnificent way to meditate, even if you're only in your own backyard. Put your concentration on the rustle of the breeze moving through leaves, or bird and animal sounds. Sit with your back against a large tree trunk to experience wonderful grounding energy.

If you find it difficult to meditate on your own, guided meditation CDs are available. They give you something to focus on to take you away from your busy thoughts and help you achieve deep relaxation. But do try to stay awake. That's *my* greatest challenge in meditation.

🐾 Connery:

As Karen has mentioned, telepathic communication is based on an exchange of information in the form of energy. Therefore, practicing methods that help clear your physical, emotional, and spiritual energy fields will aid in your animal communication endeavors. You'll be more able to hear us if you're not surrounded by mounds and mounds of baggage muffling the signal.

Karen has listed our favorite website resources for energy clearing and healing at the back of this book, but I'd like to specifically mention

EFT, the Emotional Healing Techniques®, here. (Companion animals appreciate modalities like EFT because when our humans employ them, there's far less healing work for us to do! We all have more time for enjoying life and each other's company.) Karen and I particularly approve of EFT because it empowers people to help themselves whenever they need immediate emotional support.

Remembering to breathe deeply as you do intuitive work is also very helpful. The breath can help expand your energy field, so be aware of when you're holding your breath and constricting yourself. Drinking extra water also aids the energy. And I heartily recommend turning off the TV newscasts. All that fear-vibration they promote interferes with expanding your heart energy.

Karen:

If you compare notes with other people practicing with the same animal, you may find you get different information. Part of that is that you have different ways of interpreting what you get from the animal, or you may each have made a connection with the animal at a different level. People usually think of animal communication as speaking with the personality of the animal, but it's also possible to connect at the soul level where you're speaking with the animal's Higher Self. Or you can request to speak with or scan the physical body. This can be very helpful when the animal's personality says, "Go to the vet? No, I don't need to go to the vet!" but at the physical level may be crying out for assistance.

Testing:

While it's tempting to test yourself and your poor animal companion by mentally saying something like, "IF YOU CAN UNDERSTAND ME, TURN YOUR HEAD," please don't annoy your friend. As Connery says, "Even if your cat or dog complies, you'll tend to write it off as coincidence and just keep asking for other confirming behaviors. What a bore! This is a matter of spiritual communion and trust, not a parlor trick."

The animal rarely gives any physical indication that you're having a conversation. In fact, many will relax and appear to go to sleep. This is why I actually prefer to do my consultations by telephone while looking at a photo of the animal. That way, I'm not distracted by vainly watching for some signal from the animal that I'm getting the message right. Even more important, the *animal* isn't distracted by being dragged somewhere to meet me or having me come to visit in person.

A good example of this is the time I was talking with a pet store customer who had brought one dog to meet me, but left the other at home. The dog who was physically present was so intent on the other critters and the nearby treats and toys that I could barely get a thing from him. But I had a lovely conversation with the old girl left at home. She was enjoying having the house all to herself without being pestered for playtime by the younger dog. Their human confirmed the information I was getting from her.

Looking at an animal's photo is a great way to practice as you get comfortable conversing telepathically. Try writing out some simple questions to ask, then introduce yourself to the pictured animal and respectfully ask permission to speak. Again, write down whatever comes into your mind. It may not even make sense until you talk it over with the human guardian. Should you find yourself "receiving" discouraging messages, most likely your own fears have gotten in the way and are telling you lies. You're projecting your own doubts onto the animal. The animals are generally helpful, and also happy you're paying attention to them. You'll absolutely *know* you've made contact when your face runs with tears of joy—the sign of a deep heart connection.

Testing can also occur when the human belonging to your practice animal asks skeptical questions designed to check whether you really *can* speak with the animal. This sort of thing shuts down the energy like slamming a door closed. Dawn Hayman's advice for dealing with these questions is to tell the person that you suffer from test anxiety and won't be able to answer them!

⁂ Connery:

Karen has asked me to address the topic of energetic protection as you open to do intuitive work. Yes, it's always prudent to request assistance from your Higher Power, from God. Before you begin, say a prayer for safety as you work. Ask that you may connect only with the animals with whom you're working, without any outside negative interference. Ask that your work may be only for the highest good of all concerned. Your guardian angels are only too happy to have you ask them to surround you and the animal with protective light. Trust that they extend God's loving protection to you.

God's protection makes it safe to fully open your heart. Most humans have been trained to protect their hearts by trying not to feel anything. They put up a barricade around the heart. Then, of course, though the heart is shielded, it's also restricted and confined. (No wonder you're prone to heart attack.)

☝ Karen:

Both Connery and I suggest you attend workshops in animal communication if possible. Working in a group of like-minded folks gives the energy a boost and makes it easier to transmit information back and forth between human and animal. And for the best of all options, go to a special place like Spring Farm CARES in New York state or Hummingbird Farm in North Carolina (contact information is in the resource section), where you can work with animals who devote their lives to helping you hear them.

There are many websites promoting animal communication on the Internet. One of my favorite sources for information is Penelope Smith's site, *www.animaltalk.net*. There you can find listings for communicators and classes all over the United States and beyond. Virtually everyone works by telephone as well as in person, so you don't have to look for someone in your own area, though a lot of my Midwestern clients tell me they feel more comfortable working with someone relatively local. Reading various websites can help you choose a communicator. You'll know you've found the right person to help you when you resonate with the information offered on that specific website. Other communicators were happy to give me guidance as I was learning animal communication, and that support is extremely helpful.

16 ~ The Cosmic Purr

✋ Karen:

One night in 2001, I was soundly asleep when Connery awakened me by walking up my body from my ankles to my chest. He sat firmly on my solar plexus and, even in the dark, I could sense he was staring me straight in the eye. My knee-jerk reaction: I asked him if he were hungry. No response; he just continued to sit on me, quietly purring. "Uh-oh," I thought, "Message incoming. And I'm barely awake. I'll never get it." With a sigh, I attempted to open the channels of my heart-mind and waited. Then I heard Connery's familiar mental voice. He said, "Tune in to The Cosmic Purr."

My first reaction was a chuckle—what a great cat joke, "The Cosmic Purr!" Then the profundity of the phrase struck me. The feline name for the vibration of the Universe, the music of the spheres, for unconditional Love.

As soon as the deeper meaning sank in, Connery sprawled out on me and his purr became a rumbling vibration that penetrated my chest and warmed my heart. He was congratulating me for receiving his message.

Connery:

And as we reach the final chapter, what, you ask, *is* The Cosmic Purr? The Cosmic Purr is my name for the healing essence of love. It's the vibration of God's Love, the energy that unites us all. It's living with a sense of gratitude for every moment we have on Mother Earth. We cats purr for many different reasons, to comfort ourselves, to reassure ourselves when we're nervous (like a human humming to himself), to express our love and contentment, and most of all, to offer healing to self and those we love.

Connecting with it is easy. The only thing that makes it difficult for humans is that they *forget* to make the connections, or resist allowing the connections to be made out of fear, anger, or self-loathing. We, your animal companions (and not only cats), can link you to The Purr anytime you *mindfully* connect with us. By this I mean setting aside all thoughts of paying bills, the grocery list, the malfunctioning plumbing, etc., and being fully present with your animals as you stroke them, speak with them, cherish them.

I once challenged Karen to shift her perception as she petted me. All of her attention was focused on stroking my coat in a way that was pleasant to *me*. I asked her to put her awareness on what her hand was sensing, instead. She experienced my warmth, the smooth softness of my fur, the vibration of my purr, and the way I was pushing my body against her hand. She suddenly, consciously, realized the *mutually* loving exchange in which we were engaged. This is how we connect you with God's love.

Karen:

I was feeling down, inadequate, undeserving, one morning. Connery plopped into my lap and said, "This is why we companion animals are with you—to remind you you're never really alone. We're a tangible representation of the unconditional love that surrounds you at all times: your guardian angels, your guides in Spirit, God. When you open your hearts to us and let us in, we can give you a glimmer of God's unconditional love."

My teacher and friend, Star Wolf, has a thought-provoking spiritual exercise she calls *The 30 Shamanic Questions for Humanity*. You commit to work the process with a mentor for thirty days and are given the first question. You write your response and the next day the two of you exchange answers and discuss them, and then you get the second question, and so on. After I'd completed working the questions with my mentor, Kathy, she asked if Connery would like to participate next and respond to the *30 Questions*. Of course, he was delighted to offer his answers, some of which Kathy and I found quite surprising. I started to e-mail his daily answer to my friends at Isis Cove and heard through the grapevine that Connery's essays were eagerly awaited, printed out, and passed around as soon as they were received. I'm not at liberty to reprint all of them here since Star Wolf plans to publish a book or two about the questions and wants to include Connery's responses under the title *The 30 Shamanic Questions for a Feline Philosopher*. But she has let me share with you my favorite of his answers:

Question #6: *Dictate an in-depth description of what you would like your Higher Power to be like. Be as free and open as you can possibly be. Imagine, and do not limit your picture of what the Divine should be like.*

❧ Connery:

What a fun exercise, to describe the Unknowable!

God lives in the sunshine in which I bask, and in the shadows of moonlight. See God in the orange and black of the tiger's coat, the All in One.

I see God wherever I look. In every living being, in every natural object, in every man-made creation. None would be here if not for God, the Source.

I see God in the mouse that offers itself to me and I thank God for that mouse. A Godsend for a house cat, the indoor mouse! So much more rewarding than bits of fluff or string, though God is in these, too, when Mouse isn't available.

God fills my dreams and gives me direction for my astral journeys. And I embody God in my tiger form when Karen does her own Shamanic journeys; I watch over her and assist her explorations and prod her to her discoveries.

What is my ultimate picture of God? God is the Cosmic Purr, the vibration of creation, the love/life force of all. I join my purring to the vibration of the cosmos and we are all One.

☝ Karen:

Once, while in deep contemplation, just on a whim, I asked Connery if we've known each other in past lives. The image that sprang into my mind was of the alchemist training his young apprentice. I was *not* the alchemist in that vision! Though early in his life I asked Connery if he's my teacher and he replied, "No, we're partners," I know he guides me when I have the sense to be still and listen to him. These days, we're all being asked to be alchemists. To take hold of the leaden fear that divides our world and transmute it into a flowing golden unity, bound by loving compassion. Our animal companions can help us understand at a gut level, at a heart level, that we really *are* all one. Each of us is an integral part of All That Is. Our animal friends invite us to see ourselves through their eyes, to love ourselves as they love us.

While the task seems daunting, we can be of service every time we so much as share a smile, or enjoy stroking our animal companions, or water a thirsty plant. All the little things add up. Trust that allowing ourselves to feel joy is a great gift to the world. Happiness can be as contagious as fear, so my mantra is "I choose love over fear."

Early in my professional animal communication career, I encountered a man who cautioned me, "You're not talking with animals, you're talking with DEMONS!" For once, I had absolutely no doubts and instead of convincing me, I felt nothing but compassion for someone whose fear was so intense that he was feeding power to his own nemeses with every word of warning he spoke. He also said, "You'll never hear these 'animals' speak of Jesus." Well, it's true that I can't recall any of them specifically mentioning Jesus to me, but they speak often of God and of the angelic beings they perceive so much more easily than we big-brained, "superior" humans. I sense the love radiating from the animals in my life and in the lives of my clients. All the abuse so often heaped upon them, yet virtually all remain forgiving. Such role models for us, and certainly not the message of demons.

The Purring Symphony

During a class break on one of my Spring Farm workshop trips, I went into the room housing the older cats who were either up for adoption or spending their last years as permanent residents. I sat on the couch and my buddy, "Bogey," hopped into my lap. Bogey, the big black cat with half his face and neck scarred and mostly hairless, the result of someone throwing chemicals on him. Yet he was one of the most congenial, down-to-earth critters I've ever met.

As I was stroking Bogey, the elderly orange "Tiger" climbed up and stretched out next to me (he was at least 19 years old at the time and lived several years beyond that). Bogey complained, "Hey, you came in here to see *me*," when I began to pet Tiger. Next a dainty Tortoiseshell cat walked up to me along the back of the couch. When I turned to look at her, she told me, "Now we're going to give you a *purring symphony!*" And with that, all three of them simultaneously began to purr. Surrounded in that resonating vibration, I sat there in bliss with tears in my eyes. Looking back, I realize they were blessing me with a sample of The Cosmic Purr.

🐾 Connery:

I'd like to thank you for devoting a bit of your time and attention to reading (and I hope, *enjoying*) our book. May it expand your awareness and appreciation of the natural world and cause you to look at the animals in your life with new eyes. There is far *more* wonder available to you: These stories are just a taste of the miraculous experiences that await you once you decide to go looking for them. Quiet your mind and open your heart, and we animal companions will be right there with you on that journey of discovery.

✋ Karen:

And I wish you well on that journey. I hope your life's adventure is graced with as many sages as has mine—both human and animal. Opening my heart to the animals has expanded and vastly enriched my spiritual path. I find that I'm now a facilitator in an energetic network connecting humans and their animal companions with others of like mind. By sharing our stories and personal experiences, we all link up, heart to heart.

It doesn't matter whether you decide to study animal communication or you're content to delight in the company of your animal friends the way you always have. Just remember to acknowledge the possibilities.

~ Many blessings from Karen and Connery

Resources

This is a fraction of the materials available to you. The books and websites mentioned here are those with which I'm personally familiar and are among my own favorite resources.

Animal communication websites:

www.animalshaman.com (my site)
www.springfarmcares.org
www.anaflora.com
www.animaltalk.net (Penelope Smith's site)
www.hummingbirdfarm.org
www.carolschultz.com

Recommended animal communication books:

Brunke, Dawn Bauman: *Animal Voices: Telepathic Communication in the Web of Life*
Callahan, Sharon: *Healing Animals Naturally with Flower Essences and Intuitive Listening*
Kinkade, Amelia: *Straight from the Horse's Mouth: How to Talk to Animals and Get Answers*
Reynolds, Bonnie: *If Only They Could Talk: The Miracles of Spring Farm*
Smith, Penelope: *Animal Talk: Interspecies Telepathic Communication*; *When Animals Speak: Advanced Interspecies Communication*; and *Animals in Spirit*
Solisti-Mattelon, Kate: *Conversations With Dog: An Uncommon Dogalog of Canine Wisdom*; *Conversations with Cat*; and *Conversations With Horse*
Summers, Patty: *Talking With the Animals*
Thomas, Tera: *Opening My Wings to Fly: What Animals Have Taught Me*

Energy clearing and healing:

www.innersource.net
www.emofree.com
www.masteringeft.com
www.abraham-hicks.com
www.louisehay.com

McLaren, Karla: *Your Aura & Your Chakras: The Owner's Manual*

Shamanic/Spiritual Resources:

www.shamanicbreathwork.org
www.worldtransformation.org
www.worldbalance.com
www.sandraingerman.com

Andrews, Ted: *Animal-Speak: The Spiritual & Magical Powers of Creatures Great & Small*
Chernak McElroy, Susan: *Animals as Teachers and Healers*
Froud, Brian and Jessica Macbeth: *The Faeries' Oracle*
Kohanov, Linda and Kim McElroy: *Way of the Horse: Equine Archetypes for Self-Discovery - A Book of Exploration and 40 Cards*
Sams, Jamie and David Carson: *Medicine Cards: The Discovery of Power Through the Ways of Animals*

Intuitive Resources:

www.akashicsoulvisions.com

Bodine, Echo: *Echoes of the Soul: Moving Beyond the Light*; *A Still, Small Voice: A Psychic's Guide to Awakening Intuition*; and *Relax, It's Only a Ghost*
Virtue, Doreen: *Healing With the Angels*; and *The Lightworker's Way: Awakening Your Spiritual Power to Know and Heal*

Animal Shaman Arts

P.O. Box 1998, Ames, IA 50010